DEVELOPMENTALLY DISABLED PERSONS WITH SEXUAL BEHAVIOR PROBLEMS

TREATMENT
MANAGEMENT
SUPERVISION

GERRY D. BLASINGAME, MA, LMFT

Published by:

Wood 'N' Barnes Publishing
2717 NW 50th
Oklahoma City, OK 73112
(405) 942-6812

Cover Art by Blue Designs
Copyediting & Design by Ramona Cunningham

Printed in the United States of America
Oklahoma City, Oklahoma
ISBN # 1-885473-45-1

=Acknowledgments=

I appreciate my wife and children who gave me the space and time to write this project.

I am indebted to many people who have taught me about this work. In particular are those clients who have taught me to understand their unique forms of intelligence and creativity, their yearning for a happy life, and their tolerance for those who do not understand them.

I must acknowledge the team of therapists at New Directions to Hope who work with the Developmentally Disabled Sexual Offender Rehabilitative Treatment (DD-SORT) program. Thanks to Allison Scroggins, Jim Henning, Russ York and Kasey Staley for the team effort of getting the work done. I value the shared commitment for the program and the people we serve.

I offer my thanks to Marilyn Dugan and Allison Scroggins for their time and energy invested in editorial critiques that helped shape this project.

Others have reviewed portions of drafts of the book as well. I appreciate Dave Burrell, Ron Kokish, and Niki Delson for their feedback and challenges.

Chapter two contains a list of policies that a committee of interested persons including parents, self-advocates, providers, community members and staff from agencies serving developmentally disabled persons developed for the Nova Scotia Department of Health, Community Health Promotion Fund (1998) and the Regional Residential Services Society.

Finally, thanks goes to David Wood of Wood 'N' Barnes Publishing for the support and encouragement to get this project done on time.

=CONTENTS ═══════════════

=Introduction=

HELPING a person who has a developmental disability to acquire new skills and build healthier sexual behavior patterns and relationship skills is at times a significant challenge. It requires those professionals who aspire to the task to integrate their fields of knowledge, including developmental and forensic psychology, education, anthropology, systems of service delivery, behavior modification, sex offender and victim treatment philosophy and strategies, and human sexuality education.

The author presumes that readers of this volume have had minimal exposure to literature involving persons with developmental disabilities and human sexuality. This volume is intended primarily for therapists and service coordinators with general psychology background.

Professionals and service delivery providers must develop more concrete and creative methods of intervention. There needs to be a more directive approach to managing and supervising the sexual behavior problems of people with developmental disabilities while attempting to assist them in improving their overall quality of life (California Mental Health and Developmental Disabilities Center [CMHDDC], 1999a) as well as promoting community safety. People with developmental disabilities deserve respectful care and dignified treatment.

With this resource and its accompanying program forms book, our goal is to offer a start and perhaps a roadmap to the kind of treatment the developmentally disabled client population deserves.

CHAPTER ONE

SEXUALITY AT A GLANCE

SINCE the beginning of time, humans have exhibited a wide range of sexual interests and behaviors. They are recorded in ancient hieroglyphics on the walls of caves, represented in sculpture, and addressed in ancient religious writings such as the Jewish Torah and the Old Testament of the Protestant Bible as well as in Chinese and Greek literature and classical art. The many forms and expressions of human sexuality have seemingly forever been a significant aspect of human life and relationships.

This is also true in recent history. Therapists, sexologists, and the media have literally exposed more to the public regarding the numerous aspects of human and nonhuman sexuality than has ever been revealed before. Modern American culture is fascinated with sensuality, sexuality, and erotica. Children and teens in the modern era have exposure to a tremendous amount of sexual information on a daily basis simply by watching television and subculture music videos, listening to the radio, magazines, or surfing the Internet.

Discussion, however, is often at a superficial level when one brings up the subject of sexuality in general conversation. Most people are very reluctant to disclose their personal and idiosyncratic sexual thoughts, wishes, fantasies, behaviors, or habits. Typically, discussions of sex in American culture are as if "it" is something someone else does. The anxiety related to the discussion of sexuality among many people seems related to personal insecurities and fears of abnormality. Mainstream America seems to want to be reassured of acceptance before engaging in such a personal dialogue.

However, anonymous surveys, often presented in newsstand magazines, reveal another side of America. While most people are reluctant to overtly discuss their own sexuality, they have been willing to divulge many secrets to the surveyors of our time (Michael, Gagnon, Laumann, & Kolata, 1994). Sex and sensuality have become incredible forces within our culture. Commercials on television, advertisements in magazines and on billboards use sensuality to increase sales of a smorgasbord of products, from canned soup to exotic vacations. Television advertisements for women's undergarments now sensually "exhibit" as much as the popular pornographic magazines of the 1950s.

When we review literature about human sexuality, we find that much of what is defined as "normal" is culturally determined. The evidence is clear that across time and cultures, we continue to change our minds and behaviors regarding normality. Levels of nudity; types of clothing; self-decorations such as tattoos, makeup and body piercing; sanctioned ages of consent; all vary from culture to culture (Morris, 1997). What is accepted in one culture may be illegal in another culture; what was acceptable at one point in history may be illegal now.

It is not news that American culture is replete with a wide variety of sources for learning about sexuality. Nor is it news that many people have serious difficulties dealing with their own sexuality. Sexual crimes have increasingly become the focus of the media, legislative efforts, and mental health professionals across the country–indeed across the globe. Numerous estimates proclaim that child sexual abuse, sexual assault, domestic violence and rape occur in epidemic proportions. Child sexual abuse is now viewed as a public health problem (McMahon & Puett, 1999).

On a smaller scale, social and personal boundaries are defined differently in a wide variety of familial and social settings. Conduct that is permitted or expected in family relationships is unacceptable with strangers. What is allowed in one's own home is far different from what is allowed in a public situation. What is allowed in a forest is forbidden in a city park. What is acceptable in one city may be different from what is acceptable in another. The rules in our society regarding sexuality and its varying related behaviors are many and complex.

Age and maturity are also significant factors in determining social and sexual appropriateness. Children develop their sense of sexuality and relationship boundaries through an evolving process of learning experiences. While they explore their understanding of the universe, children also explore their sexuality (Cavanagh-Johnson, 1999). Clearly, sexuality is not exclusively an adult issue or experience.

A fair amount of family life education and social relationship knowledge is required to grasp and assimilate all the sexual information made available in our times. People are wondering more often if their own sexuality is "normal." People, who have no intellectual limitations or handicaps, are often confused about the so-called changing times. Some people feel disappointed and distressed by the sexual liberalism subsequent to the sexual revolution of the 1960s, while others wish to promote an even more liberal social/sexual agenda. Managing and coping with all this information is not an easy task.

People with developmental disabilities may have more

difficulty dealing with all this. Having intellectual impairments and impoverished adaptive functioning skills effects virtually every aspect of life (American Psychiatric Association [APA], 1994). The classification of mild mental retardation encompasses approximately 85 percent of those with retardation (Alloy, Jacobson, & Acocella, 1999). In addition to inherent limitations and challenges, people with mental retardation and other developmental disabilities have been historically treated in a desexualized manner as if they did not have the same physical and emotional needs as others without developmental disabilities. In the past, those with developmental disabilities were discouraged from developing personal relationships; they were often the victims of involuntary sterilization (Alloy et al., 1999). Society and families have attempted to deny the existence of sexuality among persons with developmental disabilities.

It should be of no surprise that people with developmental disabilities are interested in sexual matters. An innate sexual drive seems just as strong among people who have developmental disabilities as it is in the mainstream population (Monat, 1982). However, adaptive functioning deficits impair one's ability to establish and maintain self-regulation, inhibitory controls, and general impulse control. These deficits can contribute to significant social and sexual behavior problems. Lack of social and/or interpersonal relationship skills can lead to frequent misunderstandings. Those with developmental disabilities may inaccurately interpret the social cues of another person with a subsequent behavior that is presumed inappropriate by intention.

To illustrate this, a case example may be useful. A young adult male with Down syndrome came to the office for his appointment. Smiling as he entered the room, he looked at an adult female who was sitting in the row of waiting room chairs where he was to take a seat. He noticed that she was returning his smile. He sat down next to her, and after a moment, reached over, took hold of her hand, and told her he liked her. Fortunately, she was a tolerant person and was able to tactfully excuse his intrusive behavior. He misinterpreted her smile as a gesture of invitation.

Another twenty-seven year old client told of his exhibitionist behaviors by describing the pornographic movies he had watched. However, when he repeated what he learned in the videos, the women and girls to whom he had exposed his genitals did not respond with the same enthusiasm as the models he had seen in the videos. Although he reported that he "had a girlfriend," observations of his social interactions revealed the extreme deficits he had regarding casual friendships, much less relationships of a more intimate nature. He had repeated his sexual misconduct all too frequently, admitting to at least twenty-five offenses and showing a preference for junior high school girls. Unfortunately, a female of any age would be acceptable to him according to his own preferences. He had tears in his eyes as he stated, "I wanted someone to love me."

Experience with people who have various forms of developmental disabilities teaches us that they have typical and normal desires for intimate and sexual relationships (Monat, 1982; Gordon & Schroeder, 1995). While they may lack certain skills, there is no paucity of desire for connection, acceptance, love or affection. Many people with mild or moderate mental retardation desire to marry and have families of their own (Gordon & Schroeder, 1995). Unfortunately, the absence of independent living skills may interfere with the person's ability to form or maintain functional personal relationships. Additionally, their opportunities for exploration and experimentation in social and interpersonal relationships are often limited due to out-of-home placement or family supervision constraints.

Intellectual impairments, poorly developed coping skills, and deficits in social opportunities may create difficulties in developing healthy and appropriate adaptive functioning. Nonetheless, people who have mild mental retardation can develop sexual behavior patterns similar to the normative population. The potential for people with moderate or severe levels of retardation is less optimistic (Monat, 1982). In fact, the lower the level of functioning, the more difficulty the client may have with understanding the abstract concepts distinguishing private versus public sexual behavior (Monat).

For people with developmental disabilities, some would distinguish between the intent of their inappropriate sexual behavior and the behaviors themselves. Some researchers refer to this as *counterfeit deviance* (Hingsberger, Griffiths & Quinsey, 1991). The causality of some sexual behavior problems among the developmentally delayed are viewed in the context of their developmental disability and the care system the person lives in rather than purely from a pathological or deviance perspective. The victims of the inappropriate behaviors would make no distinction.

Nonetheless, the offensiveness of any form of sexual misconduct is not to be minimized. Some level of treatment, system intervention, education, management and/or supervision is likely necessary (Haaven, Little & Petre-Miller, 1990; Hingsberger et at., 1991). Due to the function of negative reinforcement, problematic behaviors cannot be ignored without increasing the likelihood of reoccurrences.

The nuances of human sexuality are very complex. The fact is that many mainstream, normal adults have confusion about their own sexuality. They wonder about the impact of cultural diversity; the ever-changing sociosexual rules, values and laws; and the idiosyncratic dynamics of interpersonal relationships. Add the impact of developmental disabilities, mental retardation, and poor socialization opportunities and the puzzle becomes even more complicated. Also imposed on people with developmental disabilities are the distorted notions people, who are nondisabled and uninformed of the normality of sexual capacity, have for those with developmental disabilities.

This volume is an attempt to bring together several of these puzzle pieces.

=CHAPTER TWO==

NORMAL SEXUALITY AMONG PEOPLE WITH DEVELOPMENTAL DISABILITIES

HUMAN sexuality is indeed a complicated matter. The mainstream population appears to be confused by the diversity of sexual interests and forms of sexual expression that many people exhibit. Some people are challenged even further by the presence of developmental disabilities and other restrictive conditions.

It is evident that the expression of sexuality by a person with developmental disabilities is going to be impacted by his/her level of mental retardation (Gordon & Schroeder, 1995). Monat (1982) suggests that those with mild mental retardation can and should be treated much like the normative population, since many with mild mental retardation live independently with little need for attention. People with moderate or severe mental retardation are affected more profoundly regarding their ability to form relationships that provide them with opportunities to pursue social, sexual and/or personal fulfillment. Historically, those who are moderately mentally retarded have been viewed as trainable but not educable (Monat).

Other concurrent biogenetic and medical problems must also be considered (CMHDDC, 1999b). Many people with developmental disabilities also have additional health problems such as those related to cerebral palsy, epilepsy, Williams Syndrome, Prader-Willi Syndrome, Klinefelter

Syndrome, autism, seizure disorders, and others. These problems only complicate life further by limiting self-determination (CMHDDC, 1999a), which leads to a greater alienation from society. These are additional barriers to forming and developing intimate relationships.

The fact that a very high percentage of people with developmental disabilities experience sexual abuse as children is another complication (Haaven et al., 1990; Baladerian, 1990). Studies involving people with developmental disabilities have found the frequency of child sexual abuse victimization between twenty-six percent and eighty-three percent, depending on the study and the setting (Graham, Smailies, & Gambrill, undated). In 1985, the California Department of Developmental Services estimated the frequency of sexual abuse among persons with developmental disabilities at seventy percent (Baladerian, 1990). Graham et al. further suggest that the extent, frequency and duration of the sexual abuse against developmentally disabled children is more extensive than for children in the mainstream population. Being a person who is born with a developmental disability seems to be a significant risk factor in and of itself for becoming a victim of sexual abuse.

The effects of sexual abuse are diverse and numerous. Abuse can have a long-lasting impact depending on the timing of the disclosure, response to the disclosure, coping skills of the victim, and the type of intervention in response to the abuse (Alloy et al., 1999; Ryan, 1999). If the abuse is not reported until adulthood, time may allow the complications from the abuse to accumulate for some, while it appears to have limited effects on others (Rind, Tromovitch, & Bauserman, 1998). Some studies have found that about a third of sexual abuse victims have subsequent sexual behavior problems (Cavanagh-Johnson, 1999). While being the victim of sexual abuse

11

is not, independently, predictive of later abusive behavior, it certainly correlates with increases in the risk of sexual and other behavior problems (Ryan).

Lund (1992) reviewed several studies regarding sexuality and sexual expression among people with developmental disabilities and found that they do not always have the knowledge base from which to pursue functional, healthy relationships. People with developmental disabilities less frequently have a sufficient knowledge base regarding the basics of human anatomy, sexual functioning, sexually transmitted diseases, safer sex practices, or the social and relational aspects of human sexuality. Contributing to this problem are the parents of children with developmental disabilities who overestimate the sexual knowledge of their children (Lund). Other parents may wish to disregard or eliminate any expression of sexuality, even in their adult children.

In addition to the level of mental retardation is the ability to accept personal responsibility for one's choices and actions. Lund (1992) refers to the fact that some of the laws designed to protect people who are developmentally disabled are actually in conflict with the concept of sexual expression people with disabilities have. These laws are intended to protect the developmentally disabled clients from exploitation. However, they have led to heightened restrictions of sociosexual opportunities with other adults. Issues of competency to give consent are problematic and lead to ethical predicaments for care-providers and case managers.

An example of such a legal complication involved the arrest of a man in a residential care-home. Two men living in a care-home engaged in seemingly consensual sexual interaction. However, one of the men was legally conserved by his mother.

She objected to the activity and was determined to press charges on the other man who was unconserved. The unconserved man then faced criminal charges. Ironically, the conserved man solicited sexual activity from another resident in his home a couple of months later.

In recent years, some regions have developed policies supporting sexuality and relationships among the developmentally disabled that reside in community care settings (Regional Residential Services Society [RRSS], 1998). Such policies have yet to achieve universal support. Later in this chapter, such policies are proposed.

Depending on the living arrangements for the person with developmental disabilities, consent to express sexuality may be quite limited. For those who live independently, very few limitations, if any, are placed upon them. However, not all people with developmental disabilities have the freedom to choose their places of residence. People with conservators are in effect told where to live and with whom to live. These are decisions of large proportion and have a profound impact on the opportunities for age appropriate social and/or sexual expression and personal fulfillment.

Of course, people living in a family-member's home, residential care home, or more structured settings will have sexual urges, interests, and behaviors. It may well be that decisions regarding placement may need to consider the potential impact on the client's sexuality and opportunities for sexual expression. In choosing the least restrictive environment, one must take into consideration all the abilities and disabilities of each person (Monat, 1982).

Gordon & Schroeder (1995) reported that those persons with developmental disabilities who live in independent or semi-independent settings were prone to behave comparably to the mainstream population. Independent adult men with developmental disabilities engage in similar sexual patterns - i.e. activities and frequency - as their non-disabled counterparts. Independent adult women with developmental disabilities are reported as having sexual functioning comparable to the non-disabled *adolescent* female population (Gordon & Schroeder). Deficits of factual-information regarding the implications of sexual behavior and/or problematic issues involving contraception are problematic for the adult women with developmental disabilities.

People with more severe forms of mental retardation or other restrictive conditions would not live independently. This decreases their exposure to appropriate social learning opportunities and/or sexual and social expression. One's residential status apparently affects every aspect of interpersonal life and opportunity for personal fulfillment.

Some restrictive environments may place people with developmental disabilities in a facility that serves only same gender persons. Such placement decreases the opportunities for pursuing healthy heterosexual relationships. By default, this may increase the likelihood of sexual conduct considered sexually offensive or inappropriate by care providers, including consenting homosexual activity (Gordon & Schroeder, 1995). But all humans are sexual beings and are prone to develop sexual attraction for whomever they socialize with regardless of gender. Without age appropriate social and sexual outlets, people default to whomever they have access.

Given that care-home policies typically restrict sexual expression between residents, these persons will most likely have fewer opportunities to explore and experience healthy friendships. Care providers and case managers are compelled to extend even greater scrutiny to people who have a history of sexual behavior problems. Compounding this further are the homes that house both conserved and non-conserved residents, between whom consent becomes an extremely unlikely occurrence.

Learning, social environment and personal experience further shape, train and condition the behavior patterns of people (Gordon & Schroeder, 1995). When a person with developmental disabilities experiences a mainstream setting, his/her behavior resembles that of the mainstream population. When raised in an institutional setting, his/her behavior reflects the learning experiences and opportunities presented in that environment. Learning sexual scripts (Dacey & Travers, 1996) is an informal process for most people, with or without developmental disabilities, but it has a long-term impact on behavior. While people with developmental disabilities may be lacking certain skills or factual-information, the great majority have the same desire for social comfort, personal relationships, and fulfillment of their sexual needs in appropriate ways.

This summation would lead to the suggestion that not all sexually inappropriate behavior by persons with developmental disabilities should lead to the label of "sexual offender." As Hingsberger et al. (1991) have suggested, clearly other presenting factors (discussed in Chapter Three) influence the behavior of these individuals. On the other hand, many sexual behaviors committed by people who have developmental disabilities are indeed sexual offenses (Haaven et al., 1990; Lund, 1992). Regardless of origin or intention, the sexual behavior problems of these individuals must be addressed. Failure to intervene appropriately will subject the client and the community to the risk of further sexual behavior problems (Haaven et al.).

This of course leads to the challenging discussion of when to begin teaching and training children and teens regarding healthy sexuality. Since forms of sexually related behaviors are noted in children as young as two years of age (Friedrich, Fisher, Broughton, Houston & Shafran, 1998), it would be reasonable to imply that healthy preparatory sexuality education should begin at a very early age. The harder questions as to who should do the teaching and how much information should be given are the same for parents of children with developmental disabilities as for parents of non-disabled children. It would make sense that the parents are most likely the frontline sex educators for all children, with variations within each family system (Cavanagh-Johnson, 1999).

Many care-providers and facility administrators attempt to desexualize the clients, including considering masturbation in private inappropriate (Lund, 1992). Few facilities have policies that empower opportunity for consenting adult sexual interactions, although this picture may be improving (Ward, Trigler & Pfeiffer, 2001). Agencies, clinicians and schools working with children, teens and adults with developmental disabilities need to develop policies and protocols for assisting parents in this monumental task.

SUGGESTED SEXUALITY POLICIES

Agencies and individuals who work with people with developmental disabilities will face many decisions and dilemmas regarding sexuality and relationships. Agencies and individuals working with people with developmental disabilities, particularly with people who have sexual behavior problems, need to develop and implement reasonable policies and/or support strategies regarding sexuality, relationships and personal freedoms. Offered here

16

are beginning points for such policies and strategies involving decisions related to the client's sexual habits, choices and liberties. Having policies in place in advance reduces the tensions and potential conflicts related to such decisions.

The following are broad brush-strokes of policy recommendations proposed for elaboration, expansion and implementation by each agency, vendor, or provider serving people with developmental disabilities. Each agency will need to generate its own plan and protocol for implementing these elements to ensure that their staff will be adequately prepared to assist people who have developmental disabilities with sexuality issues. Implementation of these policy recommendations will vary and need to be integrated with each agency's mission statement as well.

Obviously, no one set of polices can adequately address issues related to individual cases and situations encountered. Minors or adults who have court-appointed conservators will require unique considerations. Implementation of these types of policies will need to be adapted to the level of abilities and capabilities of each person with a developmental disability. Implementation of these policies with conserved adults or those who have other limitations in their ability to make self-determinations will need to integrate into their legally defined conservatorship status.

The following are adaptations from policy statements offered by *Regional Residential Services Society and the Nova Scotia Department of Health Community Health Promotion Fund* (1998). It would be prudent for each agency serving people with developmental disabilities to model their own application after policies such as these, with differential application for cases involving sexual offenders or others with sexual behavior problems.

STAFF TRAINING & EDUCATION

All agencies providing services to people with developmental disabilities will provide training to ensure that their staff is competent in responding to the needs of individuals with developmental disabilities in the areas of safety, health and well being, relationships, social skills, self-esteem, and sexuality.

EDUCATION FOR PEOPLE WITH DEVELOPMENTAL DISABILITIES

Sociosexual and health education will be provided for people with developmental disabilities, regardless of the degree of disabilities. Education and support provided for parents or others responsible for educating minors empowers them to exercise primary responsibility for this education. All such education will be developmentally adapted to the client's level of understanding to provide accurate information presented in a non-judgmental, sensitive, and culturally respectful manner.

BOUNDARIES

All staff and people with developmental disabilities will receive education and training regarding establishing and maintaining professional and personal boundaries. It should be understood that it is never appropriate for a professional to have sexual relations with their client.

PRIVACY OF SOCIOSEXUAL INFORMATION & DOCUMENTATION

Any documentation in a person with developmental disabilities' file concerning sexual matters will be limited to issues of health, mental health, and safety. Communication and documentation will be respectful of the person with developmental disabilities' dignity and self-determination, treated as confidential in nature, and stored/accessed only on a need-to-know basis. Staff will receive training and periodic review of documentation practices.

PRIVACY OF SPACE

Privacy of space and time is a need for all people, allowing for independent thought, relaxation, pursuit of personal relationships, or disengagement from social pressures. Individuals with developmental disabilities will have access to private space and time within their places of residence.

PRIVACY OF PERSONAL CARE

Intimate personal care, such as personal hygiene, dressing and similar activities, for people with developmental disabilities will be conducted with the consent of the individual in a manner that is respectful of their dignity and right to privacy.

RELATIONSHIPS

Mutual social relationships such as friendships, dating and loving relationships are important components of human life and personal fulfillment. Agencies will support people with developmental disabilities in developing and maintaining relationships outside of that with paid staff members.

CONSENT FOR MUTUAL SEXUAL EXPRESSION

Consent is integral to healthy relationships and sexuality. Agencies will be mindful of a need to determine the presence or absence of consent for sexual expression and will educate clients regarding decision-making processes.

MUTUAL SEXUAL EXPRESSION

Adult sexual expressions are respectfully supported as matters of individual choice. Private and mutual sexual expression between consenting adults is a healthy and pleasurable expression of affection, bonding and normal sexuality.

SEXUALLY TRANSMITTED DISEASE EDUCATION & PREVENTION

People with developmental disabilities will receive developmentally appropriate and accurate information about sexually transmitted diseases (STDs); this includes the risks, means of transmission and recommended precautions.

REPRODUCTIVE HEALTH CARE

All people with developmental disabilities will have access to reproductive health care information and services.

MASTURBATION

Masturbation is a healthy expression of sexuality. Masturbation is respectfully supported when expressed in a way that does not intrude on others and is not self-injurious.

INTIMACY AIDS & MATERIALS

People with developmental disabilities that choose to use intimacy aids and materials will do so in a way that does not cause self-harm from inadequate hygiene, improper use, or use of unsafe objects. The acquisition of legal sexually explicit material and aids by adult persons with developmental disabilities is a right, unless otherwise defined in court orders, probation terms, or treatment program requirements. Adults will respect the private nature of intimacy aids and materials by keeping them in a private place. Like other sexual expressions, intimacy aids and materials are primarily a matter of individual choice.

BIRTH CONTROL

People with developmental disabilities will have access to developmentally appropriate information and counseling regarding birth control methods to assist them in making informed decisions.

PREGNANCY

People with developmental disabilities will have access to developmentally appropriate information and counseling required to assist in making informed decisions regarding pregnancy.

PARENTING

People with developmental disabilities will receive information and counseling to enable them to make informed decisions regarding parenting.

21

SEXUAL ABUSE

All people have the right to live free of sexual abuse or sexual harassment. All staff and developmentally disabled persons will receive education and training regarding early identification of suspected abuse, abuse prevention, abuse reporting, and means of accessing appropriate services.

MANDATORY REPORTING OF SUSPECTED SEXUAL OR OTHER ABUSES

All agencies recognize the status of volunteers, employees and/or staff members as mandatory reporters of suspected abuses. They will adhere to all local, state, and federal laws regarding reporting such concerns.

RESPONSE TO SEXUAL MISCONDUCT

People with developmental disabilities who engage in sexual behavior that has the potential of placing them in conflict with the law, or similar improprieties, will receive information and counseling with the goal of eliminating risks and sustaining the quality of community life.

THE DILEMMA OF PORNOGRAPHY & PEOPLE WITH SEXUAL BEHAVIOR PROBLEMS

There is often a significant amount of anxiety related to discussions about the use of pornography. Very diverse opinions exist regarding pornography, ranging from embracing it to abhorring it, with opinions shaped by conceptions of morality, civil liberty, and political correctness. Whether one likes it or not, pornography is a legal product, and suggesting restriction of its use is often a polarizing topic. Great anxiety is often stimulated when one suggests prohibiting a person with developmental disabilities from obtaining, possessing, or using porno-graphic materials.

Given the present discussion is focused on those who have sexual behavior problems or have committed sexual crimes, discussion of use, prohibition or some form of external control is in order. In this discussion, the focus will be on the effects on the viewer of the pornography, not on other issues such as subjugation of women or moral and religious views, although those are worthy con-siderations as well.

It may be helpful to begin with an analogous issue: alco-hol use. For some, consumption of alcohol is for social or occasional recreation purposes. For others, alcohol is a highly addictive substance, with dangerous side effects. Typically, as a person enters treatment or a support group, abstinence is expected. This expectation is unquestioned, even though alcohol is a legal substance, meaning people have a right to drink, and it is readily available for pur-chase. However, those who have a problem with alcohol, should avoid exposure to it at all costs. Its use clouds and changes the person's ability to make clear and healthy decisions and has likely contributed to problems in the person's life not to mention the health hazards involved. In these situations, it is reasonable to expect abstinence as part of the recovery process.

The question is whether it is reasonable or desirable to ex-pect abstinence from the use of pornography by those who have committed sexual offenses or other inappropriate sexual behaviors. Indeed, the question of pornography's relationship to sexual crime is a challenging one.

A very limited amount of research has been completed

on the relationship between use of pornography and sexual misconduct. This particular area is difficult to study. Other researchers and experts in the field frequently question the methodologies of the various studies that do exist.

One such study is a meta-analysis involving 74 different studies regarding pornography and its potential effects (Paolucci, Genuis & Violato, 1999). The researchers found modest connections between pornography use and the likelihood of engaging in deviant sexual behaviors (e.g. exhibitionism, voyeurism, and frottage), support of cognitive distortions endorsing rape of women, and negative or dysfunctional intimate relationships. Non-statisticians should note that correlation does not mean causality; however, correlation does indicate the two issues coexist at a concurrent time and may have influence on each other. The methodologies of this study are subject to challenge as it was not subjected to peer review.

Others have found differing behavioral relationships with certain types of pornography. Donnerstein, Linz & Penrod (1987) completed a literature review, with varied findings. They note that pornography is identifiable by several categories.

- Nonviolent, low-degradation sexually explicit materials
- Nonviolent, high-degradation sexually explicit materials
- Violent pornography
- Non-explicit sexual aggression against women
- Sexualized explicit violence against women
- Negative-outcome rape depictions

Those who use pornography are found to develop a degree of tolerance, i.e. becoming bored and less sexually stimulated with continued exposure. Donnerstein et al. (1987) also reported findings that continued viewing led toward more liberalized attitudes regarding acceptance of pornography itself and the support of its sale and distribution. In other words, viewing pornography has a tendency to change one's attitudes and social perceptions about use of pornography itself.

Viewing pornography relates to subsequent acts of aggression toward a person who had previously angered the viewer (Donnerstein et al., 1987). However, the same materials lead to positive behaviors toward a person who had previously been friendly. It appears that arousal from exposure to pornography intensifies emotional reaction. Pornography effects the viewer's mood after having viewed the material, which may indirectly contribute to pro-social or aggressive behavior choices. The determining factor is how the viewer feels about the content and the arousal produced within the individual rather than from the specific content viewed (Donnerstein et al.).

For some men, anger intensifies their sexual arousal. Research has defined that viewing nonviolent pornography does not increase violence against women (Donnerstein et al., 1987). Viewing violence against women, including nonsexual violence, may contribute to sexual aggression toward women. In other words, the type of pornography may have differential effects yet undefined by research.

Among known sexual offenders, pornography has differing effects as well. In short, research indicates that no relationship exists between use of pornography and the frequency of sex crimes or types of acts among child molesters (Abel, Mittleman & Becker, 1985, cited in Donnerstein et al., 1987). On the other hand, rapists have less sex education than non-offenders do. Research suggests that rapists may not be able to make distinctions between appropriate and non-appropriate activities viewed in pornographic materials (Check & Malamuth, 1986, cited in Donnerstein et al.). When pornography depicts violent and aggressive acts, such as rape, it is more influential than when depicting nonviolent behaviors.

Nonetheless, extensive research does not define a causal link between viewing pornography and crime. The data does imply that viewing pornography does change the viewer's beliefs and social attitudes about pornography itself. The data also suggests that for those with poor sexual education, pornography may present them with distorted ideas about sexuality, forms of sexual expression, and social behavior. For some people, viewing certain types of pornography, violent pornography in particular (Donnerstein et al., 1987), seems to influence their behavior, including aggression of a sexual and nonsexual nature.

People who surf the Internet know that it is easy to find a variety of pornographic themes explicitly depicted. The research cited predates people accessing the World Wide Web. New research needs to ascertain any differential effects of the new level of accessibility to such a variety of erotic materials. Included in these materials are images depicting any paraphilic interest imaginable, fees for cybersex service and personal chat rooms. The intensity and nonstop opportunities for immediate gratification while fully depersonalizing the concept of sexual interaction are particular dangers related to Internet pornography (Rosenberg, 1999).

People with developmental disabilities who have sexual behavior problems raise more questions when considering the use of pornography. Unfortunately, extensive research does not address potential effects specifically involving people with developmental disabilities. However, applying the information noted above may offer some conclusions. Offered here are concepts to provoke thought rather than definitive statements.

FACT: Sexual offenders, and others with sexual behavior problems, have demonstrated poor judgment, lack of impulse control, and lack of understanding regarding their sexual choices and actions.

> CONCERN: Exposure to aggressive acts in pornography may contribute to the continuation of distorted ideation and behavior. Arousal to nonviolent sexual stimuli may reactivate or reinforce a sexualized view of relationships and people, potentially placing the offender in a higher risk situation.

> SUGGESTION: Those with known sexual decision and behavior problems should reduce the level of sexual stimuli in their life while they learn and/or relearn a healthier sexual decision-making process.

FACT: Many sexual offenders, with and without developmental disabilities, have reported habitually sexualizing images, pictures, objects and people whom others do not find sexually stimulating. These materials may or may not be identified as pornography by cultural standards. Offenders also report they feel they can cope better with life after sexual activity, such as masturbation, using these fantasies.

> CONCERN: It is not possible to predict how an offender will respond to varying sexual stimuli. Those with sexualized views of people and relationships or who use sexualized thinking and

behavior as a coping mechanism, may use cognitive distortions to eroticize inappropriate targets. Pornographic materials may exacerbate such cognitive distortions and emotional reaction. Over-reliance on sexual release as a coping mechanism may inhibit the person from developing additional and more functional methods of coping and/or for expression of emotion.

SUGGESTION: Those who use sexual fantasy and/or behavior as a primary coping mechanism would benefit from developing additional strategies to cope with life issues including boredom, frustration, loneliness, anger, and other potentially unpleasant emotions. Sex is good but is not always the best response to distress or positive stress (eustress). These people may also benefit from learning how to develop more fulfilling nonsexual personal relationships to meet their needs.

FACT: People with developmental disabilities who have sexual behavior problems often have limited sex education and social experimentation opportunities.

CONCERN: These individuals may be at higher risk of acquiring distorted messages about sexuality, including distinctions between fantasy and reality, acquiring consent, women's dispositions toward sex on demand, use of force, and personal versus public behaviors by viewing pornography. Such distortions may contribute to faulty choices or behaviors.

SUGGESTION: People with developmental disabilities who have sexual behavior problems should have access to developmentally appropriate, accurate and factual information about sexuality and sociosexual relationships.

FACT: People with developmental disabilities who have sexual behavior problems often have limited impulse control.

> CONCERN: Viewing pornography may increase overall arousal and could lead to intensified emotional reactivity, both positive and negative. They may be at a higher risk for additional behavioral problems subsequent to becoming aroused, particularly if the pornography involves depictions of aggression.

> SUGGESTION: Those with impulse control problems should reduce or eliminate the factors contributing to increased agitation and irritability. In some cases, this may mean learning better impulse control skills. In other cases, it may mean decreasing use or exposure to the things that create excessive arousal, which may or may not include pornography.

FACT: People who view pornography over time develop a degree of tolerance to the stimuli.

> CONCERN: Regarding sexual offenders the question remains: if they become tolerant and bored with the stimuli, will this increase their desire to seek out opportunities for new or higher stimulation? Many sex offenders with and without developmental disabilities have reported that viewing sexually stimulating materials increased their appetite for sex and contributed to their choice to act inappropriately.

SUGGESTION: Those with known sexual decision and behavior problems should reduce the level of sexual stimuli in their life while they learn and/or relearn a healthier sexual decision-making process.

FACT: Many sexual offenders report a struggle with obsessive and intrusive sexual thoughts and/or compulsions to perform sexual behaviors.

CONCERN: Exposure to pornography or other eroticized materials may feed such obsessive thinking and contribute to the perpetuation of the offender's pattern of generalized deviance.

SUGGESTION: Those with obsessive sexual thinking need to reduce their exposure to sexual stimuli to reduce the discomfort that comes with such intrusive experiences. Medication may assist the process of diminishing obsessive sexual thinking.

The question of pornography is a complex one. There are several elements and issues involved. It has been the position of the DD-SORT program to encourage the reduction and/or monitoring of sexual stimuli during the treatment process, while reconstructing the sexual offender's understanding of sexuality and the myriad of related behaviors.

Other factors involved with an individual's decision-making process involving use of pornography include the moral and religious values of each person. As treatment providers and case managers, our role is not to dictate the moral or religious values for those whom we serve. It is our role to assist people with developmental disabilities to explore their own faith perspectives, issues of sexual comfort and/or shame, and to encourage them to make right decisions for themselves. Values clarification exercises are useful in this process.

=CHAPTER THREE=

SEXUALITY, SEXUAL OFFENSES & SEXUAL OFFENDERS

BEFORE looking at types of sexual offenses and offenders, it is important to understand some of the varied motivations for sexual behavior. The value of reviewing the literature regarding normal child and adolescent sexual behaviors is significant. Baseline comparisons distinguish the sexual behaviors of those with and without developmental disabilities. Most peoples' definition of "normal" is idiosyncratic, based on personal experience, upbringing, personal comfort, and candor in conversation.

In the normative population, not all sexual behaviors have a sexual motive (Dacey & Travers, 1996). In discussing normal adolescent sexuality, Hajcak & Garwood (1989) offer the following alternative motivations.

> TO CONFIRM ONE'S MASCULINITY OR FEMININITY: Sexual activity becomes evidence or proof of being masculine or feminine, particularly for those whose sexual identity is not intact. Conquests may serve to dispel self-doubts and insecurities.

> TO GET AFFECTION: The physical aspects of sexual behavior including hugging, kissing, and caressing, demonstrate affection. For some persons, sexual activity becomes the vehicle for - at least temporarily - receiving care from another

person. Clearly, this may lead to a lack of distinction between the expression of sexuality and affection and can have lifelong implications.

TO REBEL AGAINST PARENTS, AUTHORITY FIGURES, OR SOCIAL RULES: Becoming sexually active - particularly becoming pregnant - is a method of differentiating oneself from one's parents and establishing identity and individuation.

TO IMPROVE ONE'S SELF-ESTEEM: Being sexually active is sometimes a mechanism for falsely bolstering self-esteem. "Scoring" boosts feelings of friendship and acceptance.

TO DEGRADE OTHERS OR PAY THEM BACK: Sexual behavior is sometimes used as a tool to exert power over another person or to humiliate them. Date rape, sexual battery or coercive sex may reflect the contempt that the offender has for another.

TO DISCHARGE ANGER: Sexual behavior can be misused to express angry or hostile feelings. This exemplifies the dangerous combination of sex and aggression and can become problematic. Some teens use masturbation with aggressive fantasy as a mechanism for venting emotions, including anger and frustration.

TO RELIEVE BOREDOM: In this case, sexual behavior or masturbation is a coping mechanism, a form of self-stimulation, or entertainment. Of course, overreliance on singular coping mechanisms can lead to poor coping and inadequate social skill development.

TO KEEP A PARTNER: Some teens erroneously think that giving in to sexual pressure is a sure way to keep a boyfriend or girlfriend. Sex is sometimes the cost of maintaining a relationship.

This is not to say that adolescents do not experience sexual arousal when engaging in sexual behaviors based on these motivations. However, using sexual activities or expression to meet these types of nonsexual needs can become part of one's sexual identity, which, in turn, becomes a long-term pattern or script (Dacey & Travers, 1996).

Social learning and cognitive-behavioral learning theories suggest that pairing sexual behaviors with the needs represented by these nonsexual motives can lead to conditioned responses triggered by experiencing a basic personal need. Unfortunately, this pairing is not likely to be something the person is aware of, and by using sexual behavior to substitute for these other needs, the person will have difficulty learning other appropriate coping mechanisms for meeting emotional needs (Dacey & Travers, 1996). Such conditioned behaviors may not lead to genuine fulfillment of the original emotional need. Misguided sexual activity may contribute to poor development of self-identity, emotional self-regulation, and social and/or relationship skills.

In another study, normal children were found to exhibit numerous sexual behaviors at varying levels of frequency and at various ages (Friedrich et al., 1998). After studying over 1,000 non-sexually abused children the results showed that the observation and frequency of a child's sexual behaviors are related to the child's age, maternal education, family sexuality, family stress, family violence, and the number of hours per week they spend in daycare. The types of sexual behaviors exhibited by these children most frequently were self-stimulating behaviors, exhibitionism, and behaviors related to personal boundaries. The older the children were, the less likely their mothers would observe their sexual behaviors.

In other words, within the normative population exists a wide range of sexual behaviors, exhibited by people of all ages, beginning in very early childhood. It would appear that the propensity for sexual expression lies within all people. Social learning and cognitive-behavioral theories would suggest that the factors that lead some to misbehave sexually are based on family and social environmental contributions, learning experiences, consequences and rewards of sexual experimentation, and the opportunity for self-expression (Gordon & Schroeder, 1995; Dacey & Travers, 1996).

TYPES OF SEXUAL OFFENSES & SEXUAL OFFENDERS

There are many ways to characterize sexual behaviors. Groupings of private and public activities characterize sexual behaviors. The level of choice, consent, and participation by individuals engaging in the sexual activities characterize various sexual behaviors. Other characterizations involve the motivation of the parties involved, the level of comfort or discomfort experienced by the parties involved, and the degree of deviant preference or intent.

People with developmental disabilities tend to have deficits in several domains that affect sexual decision-making and activity (Lund, 1992). These would include sexual knowledge base, personal boundaries, impulse control, social skills, assertiveness skills, coping skills, and a sense of what is or is not potentially harmful to them and/or to others. Add this to the frequent lack of appropriate opportunities for experimentation with normal sexual behaviors, and the risk of sexual behavior problems increases, whether intentionally or not.

Consideration of the context of other behavioral difficulties and vulnerabilities respects their impact on the sexual behavior problems among people with developmental disabilities (Sherak, 2000). Sherak identifies a significant co-morbidity of paraphilia and other mental disorders such as depression or attention-deficit, hyperactivity disorder.

Sexual offenses, typically involving deviant or paraphilic behavior, involve a variety of sexual conduct. The behaviors of the developmentally disabled sexual offender population are not significantly different from the non-disabled sexual offender population (Haaven et al., 1990; Lund, 1992). Many sexual offenders exhibit multiple paraphilic behaviors (APA, 1994; Alloy et al., 1999). Abel (1995) has found that an offender with multiple paraphilias is at higher risk for re-offense.

It is important to distinguish deviant from non-pathological fantasies and/or behaviors (APA, 1994; Sherak, 2000). Of diagnostic importance is the answer to questions regarding personal distress, sexual dysfunction, and legal or social impairments (APA). Those with mental retardation or other mental/cognitive impairments, judgment, social skill, and impulse control problems, may eventually exhibit objectionable behaviors. However, in the case of paraphilic behaviors, there is a preference and/or compulsive nature to the sexual behaviors. Furthermore, an isolated behavior is not diagnosable according to established diagnostic criteria (APA), even if it were disturbing to an observer, parent or caregiver.

Paraphilic behaviors are typically socially unacceptable and regarded with some degree of repugnance (APA, 1994). These behavior patterns may or may not be the person's primary sexual outlet, depending on the individual's sexual habits. Several paraphilic patterns onset in adolescence, while some may begin in younger childhood years (APA).

Paraphilic behaviors and/or offense patterns can include the following categories. The case examples listed involve persons with developmental disabilities who exhibit various traits of these disorders.

PEDOPHILIA most often involves recurrent sexual arousal or fantasizing about and/or touching of a prepubescent child, possibly involving sexual preference for males or females (APA, 1994). Such deviant arousal is identifiably the strongest predictor of sexual re-offense against children (Hanson & Bussiere, 1996). Masturbation involving pictures of children may exemplify this deviant interest, particularly when done by an adult who would have access to adult stimuli. One such client used torn out pictures of young children in swimsuits from a department store advertisement.

Not every person who molests a child is a pedophile, nor do all child molestation perpetrators maintain sustained sexual interest in children (Abel, 1999). Some offenders with developmental disabilities have one child victim, while others have numerous victims. The incest only offenders often present sexual interest patterns similar to non-offenders (Abel, 1995). Marshall (1999) found that approximately 25% of incest offenders had recurrent sexual fantasies of children, while 40% of non-familial child molesters had recurrent fantasies of children.

EXHIBITIONISM involves exposing one's genitals to unsuspecting persons, sometimes involving self-stimulation, rubbing, or masturbation in front of the victim. Some exhibitionists prefer to expose themselves to teens or children, which may escalate the diagnosis across multiple paraphilic categories. This category of sexual behavior may also include performing sexual acts in public regardless of the risk of observation by others. A common goal for exhibitionists is to shock or surprise their victim, with the fantasy that the victim will become aroused and sexually interested (APA, 1994).

A variation of exhibitionism is that of public indecency, public masturbation or self-stimulation in a public area. This sometimes occurs without the intention of observation by others. Some who have done this behavior report masturbation behind bushes in parks, in vehicles in parking lots, in the care home transportation van, or while blatantly exposing themselves to a victim. One client reached orgasm while he stood in front of the counselor's office, masturbating inside his pants.

FETISHISM involves preferring or requiring use of particular nonliving objects in order to become sexually aroused (APA, 1994); frequently used are high-heeled shoes, lingerie, panties, boots, pictures, silk sheets, etc. Fetishism may also include sex toys or other objects used in sexual behavior. In order for the behavior to rise to a diagnostic level of concern, the object must become more important than having a human partner. A formal diagnosis of fetishism would not limit the articles of clothing to those used in cross-dressing (APA). One offender reported masturbating with girl's underwear found in his day program's job site trash bin.

VOYEURISM involves viewing or peeping at unsuspecting persons who may be in the process of undressing or engaged in sexual activity. Masturbation by the offender may or may not occur during the peeping episode. Masturbation occurs more often during fantasy or memory of the scene (APA, 1994). This behavior pattern often becomes a primary sexual outlet among more severe paraphiliacs (APA).

Some consider the inclusion and obsessive use of pornography a voyeuristic behavior (Milner & Dopke, 1997). A "model" from magazines, videos, or the Internet is fully aware of the intent of a viewer. However, there is still a blatant lack of relationship between the viewer and the object of attention. Furthermore, obsessive use of pornography tends to be secretive and exemplifies impersonal sexual gratification. Many voyeurs attempt to look up skirts or down necklines, in subtle and not so subtle ways. Endorsement for this behavior occurs in adult comedy programs on television.

FROTTAGE OR FROTTEURISM involves gaining sexual pleasure or arousal from touching or rubbing against a non-consenting person (APA, 1994). The place of contact does not need to be a traditionally defined erogenous zone, i.e. breasts or buttocks. Some offenders have reported sexual stimulation from touching a person on the hair, back, shoulder, or arm; a hand, leg, foot, hip, or other point of physical contact between two bodies can bring sexual arousal. Child victims of frottage may not realize they were touched for a sexual purpose by the perpetrator. Others report erotic pleasure from stroking the hair of staff persons in their care home. Based on incident reports and staff logs, frottage occurs frequently in residential care programs and school settings.

COPROPHILIA involves gaining sexual arousal from

involvement with feces via elimination or consumption (Milner & Dopke, 1997). Several clients have had unique fetish patterns involving use of soiled diapers or clothes for sexual arousal. Some clients used feces as a type of lubricant during masturbation but readily gave up the habit when they were educated to use a more appropriate medium, suggesting the problem was not coprophilia. On the other hand, one client frequently consumed feces during self-erotic behavior. Several sexual abuse victims have reported receiving enemas from a parent despite believing one was not necessary for health purposes.

Some people with developmental disabilities have poor hygiene skills or poor toileting habits. These are significant concerns, but are not necessarily indicative of coprophilia.

UROPHILIA involves gaining erotic pleasure from the use of the urinary stream, with or without a partner (Milner & Dopke, 1997). Subtypes of the disorder include urinating on a partner with sadistic purpose, or being urinated upon with masochistic purpose. One client reported standing outside the women's bathroom at parks so he could listen while they urinated. He reported that the sounds he heard reminded him of the woman's vagina, and he would masturbate while listening. While in placement, he reported standing outside the women's bathroom at his day program in order to be able to listen for similar sounds.

ZOOPHILIA OR BESTIALITY involves sexual contact with an animal for the purpose of sexual arousal or activity (APA, 1994; Milner & Dopke, 1997). It is typical for youngsters to be curious about sexual anatomy. However, non-experimental exploration or obvious sexual behaviors such as genital contact, oral-genital behavior, or penetration become issues of concern. Many with this disorder have multiple other paraphilias as well (Milner & Dopke).

PICTOPHILIA involves obsessive use of obscene or pornographic pictures, movies or videos (Milner & Dopke, 1997). Frequently related to compulsive masturbation, the use of sexually stimulating pictures or mental images fills some clients' obsessive thought patterns. Some clients' versions of pornography included pictures from the daily newspaper, children's pictures on dog food bags, and department store ads of children in swimsuits. Several adult clients have reported that children's television programs are sexually arousing in part because they previously watched such programs while victimizing young children.

> One such client drew his own pornographic material by drawing a picture of a penis and testicles on a flat rock. Staff found the rock in his wastebasket. He later admitted looking at it during masturbation, and demonstrated other hand drawings he used in creating his own sexual stimuli. The same offender had victimized three young boys by showing them commercial pornographic magazines and attempting to teach them to masturbate.

Related to pictophilia is OBSESSIVE OR COMPULSIVE MASTURBATION. This involves autoerotic behaviors that can develop into compulsive habits when used as a coping mechanism or outlet for emotions or tension. Some have referred to such behavior patterns as "sexual addiction." Masturbation in and of itself is not problematic when done in private and not self-injurious. Yet, some clients describe being so compelled to masturbate that they cannot get their minds off the subject until they "relieve" themselves of the obsessive thoughts through compulsive masturbatory behavior. When under such compulsive pressure, the person may lose judgment regarding when and where masturbation is appropriate, which could lead to public masturbation or exhibitionist behaviors. One female client reported masturbating at her place of employment up to five times per day. The pleasurable reinforcement subsequent to masturbation can become an over-relied upon outlet, reducing the persons' interest in learning other coping and stress-reduction skills.

TELEPHONE SCATOPHILIA involves making unwanted verbal or written expressions of a sexual nature, often involving threats or insinuations of impending sexual aggression over the phone (Milner & Dopke, 1997). This conduct is a form of sexual harassment, making it an illegal act. A number of female clients have reported receiving such disturbing phone calls from men at their day programs.

NARRATOPHILIA involves use of dirty and obscene words with a sexual partner (Milner & Dopke, 1997). Calling phone-sex service numbers is included in this category, as well as Internet chat rooms. Reading pornographic stories or having stories read to the person meet the diagnostic criteria as well (Milner & Dopke). Many clients with developmental disabilities report sexual arousal subsequent to hearing others say certain "nasty words."

TRANSVESTISM OR CROSS-DRESSING involves achieving sexual arousal or gratification from wearing or fondling the clothing of a person of the opposite gender

(APA, 1994). Some transvestic male clients incorporate shaving their legs, arms, and armpits to enhance their cross-dressing experience. Many consider this a harmless form of sexual expression. Transvestic fetishism frequently involves the use of undergarments with some clients reporting burglarizing the rooms or laundry baskets of females to whom they have access.

Children taking and/or wearing the undergarments of the other gender may risk developing problems in this area, which is behavior often observed within the normative population. Knowing the age, frequency, duration of the behavior, and response to any parental sanctions would be helpful in determining the severity or existence of a problem (Friedrich et al., 1998; Cavanagh-Johnson, 1999).

GENDER IDENTITY DISORDER in early childhood or adolescence, some youngsters develop a confusion regarding their sense of gender identification versus their assigned sexual anatomy. This is not the same as childhood transvestic behavior. Youth with gender identity disorder typically are concerned that a mistake was made when they were born, and they should have been born the other sex (APA, 1994). This is more frequent among boys. They will often report experiencing social rejections subsequent to manifestations of effeminate behavior. There is no physiological basis for the ideation, i.e. their genitalia are normally developed (APA). Homosexual interest is not necessarily related to gender identity disorder, rather psychosexual immaturity.

TRANSSEXUAL IDEATION involves an extension of a gender identity disorder. These individuals, who believe they should have been born as the opposite sex, desire to have sex change surgery to complete their transformation.

The APA (1994) estimates 1/30,000 males and 1/ 100,000 females actually seek sexual reassignment surgery. Support groups and Internet resources are available in many communities for those who identify these lifestyles as socially acceptable, contrary to the psychiatric community. Persons with this thought and behavior pattern may be sexually attracted to males, females, both, or neither (APA).

One adolescent boy indicated he wanted to have surgery to become a girl because "people are nicer to girls." This example does not encapsulate the transsexual schema, but his stated desire to become a girl was alarming to his mother.

SADISM involves gaining sexual arousal or gratification from inflicting real physical pain or injury to another person. While many mainstream couples report playful behaviors (such as tying each other up) that flirt with this category of interest, the behavior is not diagnostically significant unless real, not simulated, pain is being inflicted (APA, 1994). Rape and/or forced sexual acts often fit into the category of sexual sadism. Some offenders receive sadistic arousal from observing psychological suffering or humiliation inflicted on the victim (APA). Some clients have discussed enjoying the power and control over the victims, while others have reported enjoying the element of surprise.

MASOCHISM involves erotic pleasure gained from receiving the infliction of physical pain or humiliation (APA, 1994). The pain may be self-induced or inflicted by a partner. It may also include piercing and pinning (infibulation) (APA). Blindfolding, binding, spanking, sticking with pins, shocking, humiliating, and/or fantasizing about being raped while in such conditions are traits of masochism (APA).

HYPOXYPHILIA OR AUTOEROTIC ASPHYXIA involves erotic pleasure gained while reducing the oxygen supply to the brain (Milner & Dopke, 1997). Sometimes referred to as "terminal sex" due to the lethal risks involved with such behaviors such as temporary hanging by the neck, chest compressions, plastic bags over the head, etc. during masturbation (APA, 1994; Milner & Dopke). Hypoxyphilia is a form of sexual masochism (APA).

SEXUAL ASSAULT OR BATTERY are legal terms that may include uninvited or unwanted sexual touching or kissing, forced or coerced sexual activity, even if the two parties had previously had consenting sexual activity. Referred to as date rape, coerced sex, and/or spousal rape, these behaviors are illegal. Some frottage incidents may fit into this legal category as well. Criminal charges of sexual battery involve some less intrusive incidents of child sexual abuse.

PROFESSIONAL SEXUAL MISCONDUCT involves sexual involvement between a client and a care provider, medical or mental health practitioner, or other persons in authority over the client or supervisee. This would include forms of sexual harassment or coerced sex between two parties where one of them has some type of authority over the other. It should be questioned that any client could have truly consenting participation with someone who is responsible for supervision, controls behavior and activities, or enforces placement rules, probation terms, or conservator mandates. One study found that approximately forty-one percent of perpetrators of sexual abuse among developmentally disabled persons living in placements were service providers, not family members, peers, or strangers (Sobsey, 1994).

An individual must have recurrent sexual fantasies or behaviors that are distressing to him/herself or are socially or legally problematic in order to make a formal diagnosis of these disorders (APA, 1994). While the conduct of many offenders is not particularly distressing to themselves, the absence of consent from another person who becomes involved or the illegal nature of the behavior leads toward a diagnosis. Furthermore, some of these deviant or paraphilic sexual interests involve inanimate objects or behaviors that are not directly harmful to others. Some have argued that paraphilic behaviors done in private, i.e. personal paraphilias, are acceptable and need not be scrutinized (Hingsburger et al., 1991).

Offensive Behaviors Versus Offending Behaviors

The *behaviors* of the developmentally disabled sexual offender population are not significantly different from the non-disabled sexual offender population (Haaven et al., 1990; Lund, 1992). However, it is debatable that while the behaviors themselves are the same, the factors *causing or contributing to* the behaviors may be different.

Certainly when conducting forensic evaluations and assessing the risk of re-offending, a variety of factors must be considered. These would include identifying the factors that undermine the offender's level of control over their behavior, the level of performance and/or treatability in relation to relapse prevention, and the level of external control needed to protect past victims and/or potential victims in the community (Melton et al., 1997).

In the case of developmentally disabled persons with sexual behavior problems, the environment in which the person lives and/or has been raised is an important consideration (Monat, 1982; Gordon & Schroeder, 1995). While many have grown up with their own families, they may not have had a sufficient level of sex education or family life/relationships training (Lund, 1992).

The point at which external resources are brought in, additional factors are also brought into the case, which may not have been predicted. In the medical field, there are many instances wherein an intervention is necessary, although there may be adverse side effects. These side effects are *iatrogenic effects*. Some iatrogenic effects can be as problematic or as dangerous as the original problem requiring intervention such as medications that have carcinogenic side effects. With some psychotropic medications, other medications counter the side effects of the primary medication, as with the case of major psychotropic medications such as Haldol and Cogentin.

A potential situation for iatrogenic effect involves having non-family members provide sexuality education which leads to the question of teaching values, standards, and lifestyles. Poor training may well be an iatrogenic effect of out-of-home placement, given the systemic denial and/or suppression of sexuality of those with developmental disabilities (Lund, 1992).

Given the complications and limitations created by placement for many persons with developmental disabilities, it is important to attempt to differentiate between intentional sexual offending behaviors and sexual behaviors that are offensive and inappropriate, yet not deviantly motivated. While an intervention regardless of motivation or cause is clearly needed (Haaven et al., 1990), treatment planning considers the distinction.

47

Additionally, if service providers excuse an inappropriate behavior as having an iatrogenic cause yet there is no corrective intervention made, negative reinforcement increases the likelihood of repetition of the behavior. The danger then becomes that the inappropriate behavior develops its own self-reinforcement, and although originally iatrogenically caused, it maintains itself as an independent deviant behavior. At that point, it would not matter where or how the behavior started; it would be a potential threat to community safety or to those in the offenders' environment. Therefore, it is necessary to intervene regardless of the cause of the original behavior. Community safety needs to be the first priority (Haaven et al., 1990; ATSA, 1997). Nonetheless, there is a distinction between sexually *offensive* behaviors and sexually *offending* behaviors among developmentally disabled persons.

With the developmentally disabled population, recognition of the iatrogenic effects of the systems of care is not only reasonable but is also necessary. Hingsberger et al. (1991) proposed eleven "counterfeit deviance hypotheses." Their constructs appear to emphasize the differential between one who has done sexually inappropriate behavior and one who is deviant by preference. The concern is that some people with developmental disabilities may inaccurately become labeled and subsequently have their liberties restricted or that the system charged with caring for these individuals may fail to recognize and respond to the iatrogenic effects of the system itself. Their theoretical constructs are as follows:

- THE STRUCTURAL HYPOTHESIS: By design or default, the system of care may have failed to address the sexual expression needs of the developmentally disabled client. By developing laws and/or policies that reduce the clients' opportunities for privacy and sexual expression, the iatrogenic effect would cause these individuals to seek opportunities in settings that are inappropriate yet out of the purview of the care providing staff.

- THE MODELING HYPOTHESIS: Some sexual behavior problems are misguided repetitions or reenactments of "caring behaviors" executed by family members or staff persons. These would include clients being naked in front of staff for hygienic/bathing purposes, or corrective interventions done in invasive methods, with the developmentally disabled client viewing and later inappropriately repeating the behavior.

- THE BEHAVIORAL HYPOTHESIS: Some sexual behaviors are mechanisms to gain rapid and significant attention from family or care home staff persons. Some clients learn that the only way to get attention is through negative behaviors, and there is significant positive reinforcement for committing problematic sexual behaviors.

- THE PARTNER SELECTION HYPOTHESIS: Because many developmentally disabled people are not afforded age appropriate opportunities to develop fulfilling relationships, they may well seek out opportunities to relate to staff or available children in an attempt to develop intimate relationships.

- THE INAPPROPRIATE COURTSHIP HYPOTHESIS: Lacking in the complex skills needed to gradually move through the stages of relationship development and unable to discern the nuances of private versus public behaviors, developmentally disabled persons may become too aggressive in their pursuits of personal friendships and relationships.

- THE SEXUAL KNOWLEDGE HYPOTHESIS: Given their problems with learning through subtle social learning experiences, some people with developmental disabilities develop sexual knowledge deficits. When afforded sex education, it is often in the context of biology and body parts rather than in the context of social relationships and self-control. Some cases involve clients being given too much information to process, exciting excessive curiosity.

- THE PERPETUAL AROUSAL HYPOTHESIS: Some persons with developmental disabilities appear to be perpetually aroused due to their inability to fulfill their sexual needs in a normal way, or they may not have the knowledge or skills required for achieving orgasm.

- THE LEARNING HISTORY HYPOTHESIS: People with developmental disabilities brought up in overly protective homes or non-normative environments do not have normal learning opportunities. This may also include abuse victims or those who lack socializing opportunities to experiment with appropriate sexual expression and develop habits that are illegal or socially unacceptable.

- THE MORAL VACUUM HYPOTHESIS: People with developmental handicaps often do not comprehend the effects of their behavior on others and, therefore, do not realize they have the ability to inflict pain or discomfort on others.

- THE MEDICAL HYPOTHESIS: Some individuals may not realize that particular symptoms are the result of a medical condition that needs attention (e.g. scratching ones genitals, albeit inappropriate in social settings, may be indicative of an infection rather than an attempt at masturbation.)

- THE MEDICATION SIDE-EFFECT HYPOTHESIS: Some developmentally disabled people take psychotropic medications, which have side effects such as inhibited sexual desire or diminished ability to achieve orgasm. If these side effects are not effectively explained to the client or care giver, sexual dysfunction could result, albeit misunderstood as functional rather than as an iatrogenic side effect of the medication regimen.

Hingsburger et al. (1991) goes on to provide a corresponding system intervention to address each of the eleven hypothesized causes of the inappropriate sexual behavior, including system modification, policy modification, better sex education, staff education, and provision of counseling to address the problems. The reader will note that in these interventions for the "counterfeit deviances," it does not appear that the client is culpable for his or her actions that otherwise are sexually inappropriate. Rather, the care delivery system is faulted or challenged to make corrective adjustments.

Hingsburger et al. (1991) also define what they refer to

as a hypothesis of "real deviance" as follows:

> BENIGN PARAPHILIA: Unusual sexual practices typically done in private and not dangerous to oneself or others. Hingsberger et al. suggest that stealing underwear for masturbation is an example of this type of paraphilia. This behavior, when done by a non-institutionalized person, would not be known about and, therefore, would have no victim or be offensive to others. However, when done by a developmentally handicapped person in a supervised setting, it is inappropriate and the person is not free "to engage in their personal benign paraphilia".

> OFFENSIVE PARAPHILIA: Sexual arousal under circumstances or behaving in ways that endanger others or are offensive, such as an adult sexually interacting with a child. Hingsberger et al. indicate that due to the potential dangers involved, a differential diagnosis clarifies that a real deviance may be present. To overlook these behaviors merely because the person has a developmental disability is unfounded.

> HYPERSEXUALITY: Ruminating about sexual themes or sexual acts sometimes leaves an individual feeling controlled by these obsessions and may interfere with daily life. Hingsberger et al. suggest this type of rumination may be an indication of a physical hypersexuality and may need management with hormone therapy.

DEVELOPMENTAL DISABILITY & MENTAL AGE

The difference between chronological age and mental age is yet another complication of determining the degree of deviance and/or inappropriateness of sexual behaviors committed by a person with developmental disabilities.

Intelligence testing originally used the ratio of mental age divided by chronological age (IQ = 100 [MA/CA]) measured by tests of academic ability (Aiken, 1985), and the testing also sought to compare individual differences in the effects of common life experiences within the culture. Mental age estimates involve administering standardized intelligence tests, determining the age at which the subject of testing ceases to be able to exhibit proficiency and comparing the person's age and proficiency levels with others. The comparative level at which the testing subject is proficient is deemed his/her mental age. Much debate has occurred regarding the veracity of intelligence testing, particularly because all subjects tested did not have the same life experiences, gene pool, and socioeconomic opportunity. The presumed equality of experience in test building is questionable (Aiken).

However, when dealing with individual persons with developmental disabilities, it does become evident that many function comparatively to younger age groups. Because IQ tests are about information processing, the ability to learn, and adaptation to the environment, people with impaired intellectual functioning should not be expected to score well on measurements that are highly loaded with verbally oriented content (Aiken, 1985). By the end of their teen years, mildly mentally retarded individuals achieve perceptual-motor and cognitive skills in the third to sixth grade levels (Aiken), and they are able to learn to conform socially. Adults aged twenty-one and older are able to achieve social and vocational skills necessary for independent living; however, they may need additional support during distressing experiences (Monat, 1982; Aiken; Alloy et al., 1999).

While developmentally disabled individuals may be able to attain concrete levels of autonomy and learning, the presence of their individual learning disabilities hinders their social sophistication and relationship skills. The presence of mental retardation increases the risk of brain disorders and emotional problems (Alloy et al., 1999; Benson & Aman, 1999). When developmentally disabled persons with an IQ above 50 experience depression, they describe symptoms quite similar to depressed persons who do not have disabilities (Alloy et al.). These challenges may interfere with the integration of emotionally and socially loaded messages, particularly concerning sexuality and personal relationships.

Many challenges arise in the quest to assist people with developmental disabilities and sexual behavior problems to become better able to function independently in society. Treatment strategies need to empower those who have developmental disabilities to accept responsibility and develop understanding and culpability for their actions. Assertiveness and communication skills training will increase self-determinism and choice-making (CMHDDC, 1999a). This will require a mutual commitment from the clients themselves, their families, primary caregivers, mental health providers, regional agency policy makers, service coordinators and case managers, residential service providers, probation officers, district attorneys, medical service providers, and educators.

CHAPTER FOUR

FORENSIC ISSUES

DEVELOPMENTAL DISABILITY & CULPABILITY

The degree of culpability or level of guilt or condemnation attributed to any person who has committed a wrongful act involves several factors. Clark (1999) suggests that culpability involves the following considerations when determining whether an individual acted knowingly, purposefully, recklessly, or negligently. Criminal intent involves the offender knowing the nature of the criminal act and doing it anyway. Reckless intent occurs when the offender knowingly disregards the unreasonable risks involved with the criminal acts. Negligent intent occurs when the offender should have known the nature of the crime but never became aware of its nature. Culpability, in the legal sense, increases when there is evidence that the crime was committed "willfully" (Clark) and with knowledge of the wrongfulness of the actions (Shapiro, 1999).

A variety of factors must be considered when conducting forensic evaluations and assessing the risk of re-offense for people with developmental disabilities. These include identifying the factors that undermine the offender's level of control over his/her behavior. Another issue is the individual's level of performance and/or treatability in relation to relapse prevention. A third issue is the level of external control needed to protect past victims and/or potential victims in the community (Melton et al., 1997). The issues of undermining factors, amenability to treatment, and level of external control all interface with a client's ability to generalize treatment concepts and increase his/her level of adaptive functioning.

Culpability decreases when the offender has diminished capacities resulting from insanity, the effects of mental disorders, or other problems that interfere with the ability to form *intent* (Clark, 1999). Regarding aggressive behaviors, *intent to harm* is a concept that is difficult to apply to many people who have developmental disabilities (Benson & Aman, 1999). Because children with mental retardation are at increased risk for mental health problems (Alloy et al., 1999; Benson & Aman), the issue of culpability is significant.

Certainly not every person with a developmental disability develops a sexual behavior problem. However, several factors interfere with normal developmental experiences and social learning opportunities. These factors raise questions about the level of culpability assigned to people who have developmental disabilities. Research has not clarified whether sexual behavior problems are more frequent among people with intellectual deficits (Kalal et al., 1999). Ward et al. (2001) indicated that approximately five percent of community agency clients have sexual behavior problems. Extensive research has identified that the cognitive distortions of persons with intellectual disabilities are not significantly different from those of mainstream offenders (Kalal et al.).

Social restrictions, alienation and discrimination create significant learning barriers for many people with developmental disabilities. Opportunities to mingle with other people their own age are under the control of their families and caretakers. For example, parents or caretakers are highly unlikely to allow a youngster to flirt or make sexual advances in front of them with age-mate peers. Therefore, the comfort level of parents and caretakers limits opportunities for age-appropriate social experimentation and for acquiring social feedback. Many people with developmental disabilities have experienced shunning and avoidance by non-disabled persons (Alloy et al., 1999).

Normal learning opportunities that promote development of awareness or understanding of the nuances of emerging sexuality and social behaviors are often lacking. Frequently, parental biases about the childlikeness and need for protection of their developmentally disabled youngster interfere with normal development. The heightened levels of supervision by teachers or others in public settings often impose stricter rules on children with developmental disabilities.

Because of these limited opportunities, the individuals are often in social situations where they are chronologically older than their peers and/or playmates with whom they are socializing. The mismatch of ages is ignored when sexual curiosity, interest, arousal, and desire converge with opportunity. The person may view his/her younger associates as the appropriate group with whom to interact, play and experiment. This situation may well be the training ground for what Hingsberger et al. (1991) referred to as inappropriate partner selection skills. Some individuals have learned to relate to children as their mental and social age-mates, making it very difficult to ascertain whether their sexual activities with children are a product of deviance or socialization.

Some people may consider this a mute point. If the developmentally disabled person has engaged in sexual behavior(s) with a child, s/he needs intervention to stop the behavior from occurring again. Too often, when a court does not find the individual culpable or guilty, intervention is not considered. Only fifteen percent of people with developmental disabilities in community-based programs that have engaged in sexually inappropriate or offensive behaviors experience incarceration (Ward et al., 2001). In other words, there appears to be a lack of accountability and formal intervention for those with developmental disabilities and sexual behavior problems.

The most ethical action to take in evaluating the sexual behavior problems of those with developmental and learning disabilities is to first consider the people rather than the diagnostic label (CMHDDC, 1999a). Other important factors include their living and learning environments (Lund, 1992). Another consideration is the possibility of iatrogenic factors contributing to the inappropriate sexual behaviors similar to those noted by Hingsberger et al. (1991). Forensic evaluations also need to determine the level of criminal thinking or mental state at the time of the offense (Shapiro, 1999). Culpability is ultimately a courtroom decision, but it may also represent a number of issues relevant to treatment.

COMPETENCY TO STAND TRIAL

A related issue for those with developmental disabilities is that of competency to stand trial. A person who is not competent to stand trial is one who is unable to participate or assist in his/her own defense due to a mental or physical disorder or retardation (Roesch et al., 1999). Competency evaluations are complex in nature, requiring expert knowledge of both clinical and legal issues.

The outcome of such an evaluation for a person with mental retardation or other mental disorders can determine several issues. First, a determination must be made as to the individuals ability to consult with his/her attorney with a reasonable level of understanding. A second issue is whether the individual has a reasonable level of understanding of the factual issues involved with the legal proceedings (Roesch et al., 1999).

The entire context of the individual's circumstances needs consideration, not just the presence of the developmental disability. Contextual factors include the following:

- The capacity to understand the relationship between the charges and any existing evidence
- The ability to relate and communicate with a particular attorney
- The ability to reasonably assist the attorney in one's own defense
- The ability to comprehend the nature of the legal proceedings
- The ability to understand the potential outcomes of the legal proceedings (Roesch et al., 1999)

Everington (1990) developed the Competence Assessment for Standing Trial for Defendants with Mental Retardation (CAST-MR). The CAST-MR is a specialized tool for competency evaluations developed for people with developmental disabilities (Melton et al., 1997; Roesch et al., 1999). The tool is a fifty-item procedure using multiple-choice options. Its vocabulary and syntax are at the fourth grade reading comprehension level. The CAST-MR also includes concrete information about the legal system. Outcome study data indicates that not all with the same IQ score have the same competencies (Melton et al.).

A variety of other forensic competency tools are available, but are not as specialized as the CAST-MR (Roesch et al., 1999). Competency evaluations are complex. The evaluations take into consideration the individual's mental health, mental abilities, and capacity to comprehend complex legal issues. The court makes the ultimate decision regarding competency–not the examiner or the tools employed (Melton et al., 1997).

POLYGRAPH EXAMINATIONS FOR THOSE WITH DEVELOPMENTAL DISABILITIES

Polygraph machines, now computerized, measure variations in three physiological domains, i.e. heart rate, blood pressure, and electro dermal activity, concurrent to the person being asked a series of questions (Abrams, 1989; Melton et al., 1997). Expert opinion or legal facts cannot be based solely on polygraph findings (ATSA, 1997), in part due to the lack of replicated scientific evidence regarding the validity of the procedure (Melton et al.; Blasingame, 1998). The utility of the use of polygraphy as an investigative tool is indisputable (Iacono & Patrick, 1999). In reality, there is no such thing as a *lie detector* (Blasingame; Iacono & Patrick). However, the procedure is very useful in leveraging information from the person before completing the examination. Many criminals have admitted to their crimes after failing a polygraph examination (Iacono & Patrick).

For many years, sexual offender treatment programs have utilized polygraphy as a treatment tool (Abrams, 1989; Edson, 1991). Polygraph examinations are routine to encourage honest and full disclosure of historical events, but only when protocols prevent the risk of further incrimination (Edson; Blasingame, 1998). The polygraph is a useful treatment tool but is not a determiner of legal facts (ATSA, 1997).

Comprehension of the polygraph questions, the culpability issues, and the feared consequences if one were to fail the polygraph examination are of interest to those working with developmentally disabled persons. Intellectual deficits and comprehension problems can be caused by organic brain dysfunction with various etiologies (Abrams, 1989). Further complicating the process is the issue of clarifying *intent.* Culpability for behavior is different from admitting to the behavior. Polygraph questions with the mainstream population avoid the issue of intent; rather, they solicit admission of behavior (Abrams; Blasingame, 1998).

Only one formal study has been done involving efficacy with persons who have mental retardation (Abrams, 1989). Abrams' study, performed in 1974, included sixteen subjects, nine of who had IQ scores at or below 64. All of those subjects were found un-testable. The results of those who were tested suggested accuracy at 71% for those whose IQs were between 65 and 80. These data do not support using the polygraph on persons whose mental age is below twelve or on adults identified as mentally retarded (Abrams).

Based on the research available, those with intellectual deficits measured by IQ scores below 65 are clearly not appropriate candidates for a polygraph examination. For those individuals whose IQ estimate is at or above 65, the polygraph would be questionable at best. Individual cases may fare well due to the placebo effect of preparing for a polygraph examination (Blasingame, 1998). In general, polygraph testing is not an acceptable treatment tool for persons with developmental disabilities, and it clearly should not be used in legal proceedings.

TREATMENT FOR THOSE IN DENIAL

Sexual offenders in denial represent a significant dilemma

for treatment providers. Therapists generally begin the sexual offender's treatment program by focusing on admission and ownership of a sexual offense, sexual misconduct or pattern of deviance. Denial creates a predicament when an offender claims innocence despite contrary evidence. Therapists typically assume that a person can only accept responsibility for change when the person admits there is a problem (Schlank & Shaw, 1996).

Maletzky (1996) summarizes that treatment with mainstream offenders in denial can have some benefit. A percentage of offenders eventually make some degree of admission. He also suggests that a majority of deniers who complete treatment irrespective of denial are successful at avoiding re-offense. Unfortunately, Maletzky also notes that these conclusions are based on limited data from small and even unpublished studies, weakening the argument.

Schlank & Shaw (1996) describe an approach used in a small study for breaking down denial. Their approach used traditional methods as well as paradoxical interventions and positive reinforcement for admission of responsibility for the sexual offenses. In the course of a sixteen-week group, they found that half - i.e. five of ten subjects - admitted their guilt.

Polygraph testing is a very useful component in breaking down denial among mainstream offenders in confrontational treatment groups (Blasingame 1998, 1999b). However, as noted above, this would not likely be a suitable strategy for the majority of offenders with developmental disabilities. The ethics of deceiving a developmentally disabled person by making him think he will be taking a polygraph examination are questionable.

Tough & Hingsberger (1999) suggest that sexual offenders

with developmental disabilities who deny the offense despite contrary evidence can still benefit from therapy. They make a good case for addressing other skill deficits through a variety of social and life skill interventions. They further recommend teaching relapse prevention skills while focusing on how the offender became subject to the accusation. They suggest building rapport and gradually confronting the offender with related issues that are high risk factors. Tough & Hingsberger suggest the process leads to behavior changes despite the non-admission. However, some would question the rationale of better equipping a sex offender in areas that may be misused for sexual exploitation. Without client commitment toward redirecting their sexual activities, skill enhancements may be counterproductive.

Clearly, denial can come in many forms or levels (Schlank & Shaw, 1996). These levels include various minimizations and lack of awareness of the impact of the abuse behaviors. Another variation involves claiming a lack of intent to harm but admission of the actual behavior. Distorted versions of how the offense happened, i.e. "it was an accident," are also common. During the course of treatment, such distortions are typically subject to examination and modification.

However, treatment for a person in absolute denial of a sexual offense or criminal act is a difficult issue. The offender could enter a treatment program with therapist expectations of an admission and acceptance of responsibility for change. Alternatively, he returns to court and faces potential punishment. An ethical consideration is involved when an individual who claims to be innocent enters in a treatment program that will expose him to a variety of deviant individuals and ideas. Alternatively, should the offender who claims innocence be referred to an attorney to attempt a retrial of the case?

63

Since therapists are not judges or juries, legal fact-finding is not the role of a treatment program. This is particularly true of a community-based program involving a grant of probation in deference to sending the person to prison for the crime. Even more problematic are cases in which the defendant plea-bargains with a guilty plea or a no-contest plea and then enters a treatment program and attempts to retry his case in the treatment program.

Denial and compelling a person to make an admission among those with developmental disabilities adds another challenge to the legal and ethical dilemma. Not forcing someone to incriminate himself (Schlank & Shaw, 1996) when he has no immunity or legal protection is an issue. Additionally, culpability issues may interfere with the process of accepting responsibility for those who have developmental disabilities.

Another issue would be discerning whether education about relapse prevention will have the same treatment effect on the person or his lifestyle as if he owned genuine responsibility for personally applying the information in a therapeutic process of change and growth. Education and cognitive-behavioral therapy are not the same even though therapy involves learning and educational processes. The research to date does not define the benefits of education alone in relapse prevention efforts (Marques, Nelson, Alarcon & Day, 1999).

While there is no good, singular solution to this dilemma, the data from the Hanson & Bussiere meta-analysis (1996) suggests that denial may not have a correlation to re-offense. Perhaps being accused, caught, or arrested and charged is a sufficient wake-up call for some individuals.

Regardless of one's position on the issue of treating deniers, many such individuals do enter treatment programs.

Some make admissions, while others travel a difficult path through a program on an "as if" basis. Nonetheless, guilt and innocence should be matters for a judge and jury to decide. A number of deniers enter treatment programs compelling us to continue to be creative and innovative in our treatment approaches as well as to pursue differential data clarifying the treatment strategies best suited for this subgroup of offenders.

RECIDIVISM OF SEXUAL OFFENDERS & TREATMENT EFFECTS RELATED TO INTELLECTUAL DEFICITS

It is a common fear and belief that all sexual offenders will re-offend. Predicting recidivism has historically been an inaccurate skill. Prediction by individual practitioners is only slightly more accurate than random chance when only using unguided estimates or clinical judgment (Hanson & Bussiere, 1996).

The most recent data suggests that the overall sexual re-offense rate among known sexual offenders is 13.4%. Among child molesters, the re-offense rate is 12.7%. Among rapists, there is an 18.9% re-offense rate (Hanson & Bussiere, 1996). By comparison, the re-offense rate for nonsexual violence is at 12.2%, while the rate for any form of recidivism is 36.3%. Hanson & Bussiere found that among child molesters, recidivism rates were lower for incest offenders (4%) than for pedophiles with boy-victims (21%).

In recent years, brief actuarial scales have been developed to assess the risk of recidivism among sexual offenders (Hanson & Bussiere, 1996; Hanson, 1997). As unstructured clinical judgment has had limited accuracy in predicting recidivism (Hanson & Bussiere), the development of the actuarial scale has been received with enthusiasm in the sexual offender treatment provider community.

Hanson & Bussiere (1996) completed an extensive meta-analysis of sixty-one studies regarding sex offender recidivism. They examined sixty-nine potential predictors of sexual offense recidivism, thirty-eight predictors of nonsexual violent recidivism, and fifty-eight predictors of general (any) recidivism, with a total sample size of 28, 972 sexual offenders. They found the strongest predictors of re-offense are the presence of patterns of sexual deviancy identified by measurement of deviant sexual arousal and/or prior sexual offense histories, histories of treatment failures, and histories of general criminality. Those who were more likely to re-offend had victims who were male and/or unrelated to the offender.

Given the number of variables identified in the 1996 meta-analysis, Hanson (1997) used sophisticated statistical procedures to analyze multiple factors and determined that four domains would allow for a highly accurate classification. The four domains are prior sexual offenses (other than the current, index offense), age below or over 25, victim gender, and relationship to the victim. Based on the data, comparisons can be made for those with similar histories, using estimated re-offense rates based on those classifications. The resulting matrix was re-administered to 2,592 cases across a number of settings. The outcome was relevant for diverse groups of sexual offenders (Hanson).

The screening tool, *Rapid Risk Assessment for Sexual Offense Recidivism* (RRASOR), generates moderate classification of risk accuracy far better than clinical estimates. The statistical system analyzed sixty-nine variables regarding co-relationship with events of re-offense. A rating closer to +1.0 is most desirable, a rating of zero

(0) implies no correlation, and a rating below zero (i.e. – 1.0) implies a reversed correlation. The higher the rating above zero, the more the characteristic co-relates with people in a classification group with a known re-offense. The subsequent data resulted in four domains identified as the most potent combination of factors in estimating risk of recidivism. Based on the four factors, the RRASOR correlated .27 with sexual recidivism, compared to prior sexual offense at .20, any deviant sexual preference at .22, failure to complete treatment at .17, low motivation for treatment at .15, never married at .11, and any male child victims at .11.

Only one factor had a stronger accuracy level than the RRASOR score. Objectively measured sexual preference for children accomplished by the use of phallometric assessment correlates to re-offense at .32 (Hanson, 1997). This is the strongest factor of the sixty-nine factors reviewed in the 1996 meta-analysis research process.

The RRASOR is not for use as a singular tool in assessing risk for recidivism (Hanson, 1997). However, the data does suggest that the brief actuarial scale is more accurate than unguided clinical judgment. This would imply that changing the estimated risk classification should only be done with conservatively established, empirically guided factors that will add to the veracity of the risk estimation. Examples of such items would be a history of treatment failure, lack of motivation to change, diagnosis of antisocial or other personality disorders, or a chronic criminal history–all factors identified in the meta-analysis (Hanson & Bussiere, 1996).

Low intellectual functioning was one of the sixty-nine variables assessed in the 1996 meta-analysis. Nine of the studies involving 5,651 offenders were reviewed, making the meta-analysis data and the RRASOR applicable to the developmentally disabled population (Hanson, 2000, personal communication). The correlation of the domain of low intellectual functioning to re-offending was at .09, with significant variability across the studies. This correlation level would reflect a relatively small effect, particularly when compared to the higher-ranking risk factors. In general, correlations below .10 are nonsignificant as they would have limited practical utility across settings (Hanson, 1997). Compared to the overall RRASOR score correlation, the intellectual deficit correlation with re-offense is very small. These data suggest that people with developmental disabilities are not inherently at a higher risk than mainstream offenders. Having developmental disabilities does not play a significant role in sexual re-offense.

The Hanson & Bussiere (1996) meta-analysis also identified areas, commonly thought of as related to recidivism, that were not substantiated in the study. These include general psychological dysfunction, depression, anxiety, social skills deficits, brain damage, being biologically related to the victim, degree of sexual contact, victim empathy deficits, denial of sexual offense, alcohol abuse, and having been a sexual abuse victim as a child. Length of treatment does not correlate with reduced re-offense rates, based on data from four studies, two of which included persons with low intellectual functioning.

Based on the actuarial data, Hanson reports that approximately eighty percent of sexual offenders are in the classification of moderate to low risk for re-offending (Hanson, 1997). For those obtaining lower RRASOR scores, the recidivism rate is less than fifteen percent within five years, within their data sample. They also identified approximately seven percent of offenders with a re-offense risk of fifty percent or more. Despite the risk classification accuracy for the RRASOR, Hanson cautions against using it as an exclusive tool. Hanson recommends its utilization within a comprehensive evaluation process.

Sexual offenders are not alike. As a heterogeneous group, their types of offenses vary. In a review of related literature, Mander et al. (1996) note several other studies that have identified that incest offenders re-offend at a frequency of 7% while pedophiles re-offended at a rate of 19%; treated pedophiles re-offend less than untreated pedophiles. Mander et al. suggest that re-offense rates may vary based on the type of treatment provided to the offender.

One prison-based study, involving a relapse prevention focused program, included academic level in its data. Mander et al. (1996) found that those with less than a high school education fared less favorably in their program. Sixty-seven percent did not continue treatment through completion of their prison sentence or the treatment program. Outcome data indicates that those who participated in any amount of treatment had a better survival rate - i.e. lower re-offense rate - than the comparison groups. Treated offenders survived longer in the community without a re-offense. If they did re-offend, it was after a longer time following discharge.

Mander et al. (1996) identified that the amount of treatment and stage of advancement in the treatment program relate to survival in the community. Nearly half (45%) of their offender subjects were in treatment for about a year, with an average length in treatment of 17 months. These data imply that the longer the offender is in treatment, the greater the benefit in terms of lower re-offenses. For those with less than a high school education, 9.7% achieve the advanced stage at discharge, 20.7% achieve the intermediate stage of treatment at discharge, and 64.1% remain at the beginning stage at discharge. Unfortunately, their data does not indicate specific re-offense rates by educational level.

The extent of risk reduction due to cooperation with treatment and community supervision is yet unknown; although, low motivation and supervision failures correlate with re-offense (Hanson & Bussiere, 1996). A question often raised involves the relationship of denial and low motivation for treatment. The overall implication is that offenders who are active participants in addressing their own deviance appear to be at lower risk when compared with offenders who do not accept such responsibility.

This is a similar finding to Haaven et al. (1990) specifically related to offenders who have developmental disabilities. The latter situation involved hospitalized offenders with developmental disabilities in a specialized inpatient sexual offender treatment program. Nearly half of the patients participated in the specialized program for approximately one year, while more than half were returned to the "parent institution" due to termination, subsequent behavior problems, and/or voluntary termination. The re-offense data suggested a modest treatment effect; 23% of sexual offenders re-offended while their overall population had general criminal re-offenses at 44%. The sexual offender-specific treatment program proves effective despite the short duration of the treatment program of a year or less (Haaven et al.). Haaven et al. report that those who remained in treatment longer received greater benefit, evidenced by a lower re-offense rate.

NON-ADJUDICATED CASES

Ward et al. (2001) estimate that approximately five percent of persons with developmental disability engage in some form of sexually inappropriate behavior. People who have developmental disabilities often do not face adjudication for their sexual misconduct (Schwartz, 1999). Only fifteen percent of a community-based sample had ever experienced incarceration (Ward et al.). Regardless of why this is true, the reality is that most people with developmental disabilities do not face the same level of consequence for their actions.

Nonetheless, some community-based treatment programs integrate these individuals into their programs (Ward et al., 2001). The movement toward de-institutionalization of people with developmental disabilities effects placement decisions for those who have sexual behavior problems. The adjudication of many persons with developmental disabilities involves referral to a regional case management agency. Those under conservatorship often live in community-based care homes. Community-based programs by necessity integrate non-adjudicated offenders within their programs.

Not all people with developmental disabilities experience adjudication; however, there is a significant danger that their needs are not met. Thirty-seven percent of community-based programs do not serve those with sexual behavior problems (Ward et al., 2001). Eighty-one percent of the respondents in the Ward et al study indicated the services in their regions were inadequate to serve the people with developmental disabilities who have sexual behavior problems. Clearly, communities need to encourage treatment programs and providers to enhance their expertise and range of services for this underserved population.

=CHAPTER FIVE=

ASSESSMENT & EVALUATION

THE unique needs of those who are developmentally disabled and/or learning disabled include numerous issues: mental retardation, deficiencies in processing and recalling information, socialization restrictions, deficits in communication skills, and a variety of medical and behavioral problems (Alloy et al., 1999; Seghorn & Ball, 2000; Sherak, 2000). Parental and caretaker limitations and frustrations further complicate family life, sexuality education, and socialization opportunities (Lund, 1992). These factors complicate the decision-making process regarding distinctions between sexually offensive behavior, sexual offending behavior, and sexual deviance. Treatment planning and systematic interventions are based on the initial evaluation, making assessment a very important part of the process.

Another area of concern, as noted elsewhere, is the difference between chronological age and developmental age. Adults with mild mental retardation, who comprise 85% of the developmentally disabled population (Alloy et al., 1999), function cognitively at the developmental levels of latency and early adolescence (Aiken, 1985). Therefore, clinical assessment and treatment interventions need to be tailored to the concrete and specific learning level of the individual. Some have pejoratively referred to this as a "dummied down" model. It is more appropriate to recognize that the challenge of the treatment providers is to deliver therapy at each client's level of functioning, regardless of chronological age, mental age, organicity, under-socialization, or developmental level of functioning and ability (Blasingame, 2000b).

Sexual behavior problems and sexual abuse are unfortunately frequent concerns among persons with developmental disabilities. Sexual abuse of developmentally disabled children occurs at a significantly higher frequency than among the mainstream population (Baladerian, 1990). Certainly, sexual misconduct among developmentally disabled persons occurs in a similar fashion to the non-disabled offender (Haaven et al., 1990; Lund 1992). Those with developmental disabilities can and do have other concurrent - or "dual" - diagnoses as well (Haaven et al.). Some recognize that sexual misconduct among the developmentally disabled population may have divergent motivations or causes (Hingsburger et al., 1991). Nonetheless, inappropriate sexual conduct has a negative impact on the victim and the offender regardless of the mental status of the offender or their motivation for sexual misconduct.

It is not a question of whether or not to intervene, but rather, what type of intervention is appropriate. In order to develop relevant treatment plans that address the varying needs of the developmentally disabled person with a sexual behavior problem, a comprehensive assessment needs to be completed.

COMPREHENSIVE PSYCHOSOCIAL & CLINICAL ASSESSMENTS

A collaborative relationship between the treatment program staff and the referring agency service coordinators is vital (Haaven et al., 1990) in order to facilitate the communication of case history and collateral file information in advance of the evaluation.

The types of file information needed are fairly broad in range, including early social histories, academic and school testing, school behavioral concerns, child protective services and/or police reports, court reports, civil commitment reports, leisure activities and recreational interests, index (present concern) incident reports, medication history, and treatment history. If the client has resided in institutional or residential care, summary information about in-home and out-of-home placement functioning will also be helpful in determining any behavioral problems of a pervasive nature. Indeed, many of the developmentally disabled clients' victims may be other care home residents. The evaluator needs to have access to this full range of background information in order to perform a comprehensive evaluation.

All too often, clinicians are obligated to work from an information deficit regarding developmentally disabled clients. Community-based treatment programs in particular need to have thorough documentation, given an offender's potential access to children and/or other vulnerable persons in the care home and adult group home systems. Early awareness of deviant interests, poor social judgment, lack of boundaries, or other risk factors can assist in treatment planning, case management, and community supervision. Of course, community safety is viewed as the highest priority (ATSA, 1997).

The initial assessment of developmentally disabled sexual offenders includes several phases: records review, clinical interviews, completion of various psychological surveys, and use of screening instruments. The following are descriptions of the assessment tools utilized within

the Developmentally Disabled Sexual Offender Rehabilitative Treatment (DD-SORT) program (Blasingame,
1994a; 2000b). There are too few tools developed specifically for persons with developmental disabilities. We
recommend consideration of the outcome data and cautious application regarding congruence with the known
histories of those under evaluation.

As many developmentally disabled adolescents and adults
are poor historians and reporters, parents and/or other
caretakers should participate in clinical interviews. Additionally, it is important to assist the clients in completing
several questionnaires and surveys. In the DD-SORT program, we use the Abel Assessment for Sexual Interest
(both computer and adolescent questionnaire portions),
the Jesness Inventory, the State-Trait Anger Expression
Inventory, the Life Facts Sexual Knowledge Screening,
and other self-report questionnaires and/or surveys to
elicit information from the client.

Additionally, depending on the age and needs of the client, parents or caretakers may need to complete such
information surveys as the Child Sexual Behavior Inventory (Friedrich, 1998), the Child Sexual Behavior Checklist-revised (Cavanagh-Johnson, 1998), the Parental Concern Inventory-Revised (Blasingame, 2000a), or the Adult
Behavioral Concerns Inventory (Blasingame, 2000c).

Being a sexual offender or person with a developmental
disability is not the only factor or issue to address in the
assessment process. It is important to explore the
person's life from a holistic perspective. Comprehensive
mental health evaluations should include the following:

- Review of available records, including prior treatment efforts, police reports, medical records, psychological evaluations, etc.

- Assessment of the client's developmental status, including level of mental and social functioning, cognitive schemata and self-esteem

- Assessment of the client's emotional and behavioral symptomology

- Assessment of the client's family environment, including members of the family and household, living conditions, economic status and resources of the family, level and degree of support available for the client and treatment process, and common cognitive schemata used by family members

- Assessment of the relationship between the offender (or person with inappropriate sexual behaviors) and the victim(s) involved, including effects on other family members

- Assessment of the client's relationship with other family members, including a spouse (if applicable), siblings, or significant others who also have a relationship with the victim(s) in the case

- Identification of the client's unique strengths, weaknesses, vulnerabilities and personal resources, including learning styles and creativity

- Assessment for the need to refer for medical or psychiatric assessment, including whether pharmacological intervention may be indicated

- Assessment of the need for further, more technical, evaluation of neurological, audiological or visual testing

An exceedingly high number of people with developmental disabilities are sexual abuse victims; some estimates indicate upwards of 70% (Baladerian, 1990). This may have a significant impact on the sexual development of many children with developmental disabilities and needs to be included in the broader assessment regimen.

As the DD-SORT program is a community based treatment program for people with developmental disabilities who have sexual behavior problems, previous psychological testing to determine eligibility for services has been completed by the time the client is referred for sexuality issues. Therefore, psychologists have already made the initial diagnosis of mental retardation and/or learning disabilities based on traditional intelligence measurements when the referrals reach our program. Clients who have enrolled in the DD-SORT program have mild and moderate mental retardation, with FSIQ's ranging from 42 to 70. For those with moderate mental retardation, testing outcomes are suspect as treatment begins, with the therapists looking to ascertain the veracity of the outcome data.

As previously noted, culpability involves identifying the factors that undermine the offender's level of control over his/her behavior, his/her level of performance and/or ability in relation to relapse prevention, and the level of external control needed to protect past victims and/or potential victims in the community (Melton et al., 1997). The initial assessment should define the client's level of culpability and sexual maturity/knowledge, amenability to treatment, mental health issues, treatment plan and methodologies, and recommendations for community supervision and milieu management issues.

MEASURING SEXUAL DEVIANCE

Over the years, empirical research has pointed to the fact that the presence of deviant sexual arousal involving children is predictive of risk for sexual re-offense (Abel, 1995; Hanson & Bussiere, 1996). These are certainly components of any diagnosis involving paraphilias, as discussed in Chapter Three.

Phallometric testing in the form of penile plethysmography has been a tool used in assessment and treatment of sexual deviants for some time (Johnson & Listiak, 1999). There are professional guidelines for this procedure (ATSA, 1997). Some consider plethysmography too intrusive a procedure as it requires actual penile measurement, and until recent years, it had limited standardization of the stimuli used. The client is fitted with a strain gauge band on his penis, as the plethysmograph involves measurement of penile enlargement concurrent to the viewing of or listening to stimuli designed to solicit sexual arousal from various themes, both normal and deviant. Plethysmography assessments focus on measuring responses to child or adult themes (Seghorn & Ball, 2000).

Plethysmography is useful with developmentally disabled males and is effective in ascertaining sexual arousal patterns (Haaven et al., 1990; Seghorn & Ball, 2000; Haaven & Coleman, 2000). While there is no specific research on the use of the plethysmograph with persons with developmental disabilities, programs using it adjust the administration protocol to allow more adaptation time between slides of stimuli and making sure the client understands the instructions. With mainstream offenders the research often uses control groups to compare treatment tools although there is no such control group developed for plethysmography with developmentally disabled persons. Some programs perform pre- and post-treatment phallometric assessments to assess change of arousal patterns over time, particularly programs that use behavioral interventions to modify sexual arousal patterns during treatment.

Phallometric testing is a highly reliable tool, with a few notable exceptions including potential non-responsiveness in the test situation (Blasingame, 1996; Seghorn & Ball, 2000). Nonetheless, the plethysmograph procedure is a well-researched tool that has held favor for many years. While its outcome identifies the domains of sexual arousal in the client being tested, that outcome should never be used to determine legal facts or guilt (ATSA, 1997).

The Abel Assessment for Sexual Interest (AASI) is a less intrusive alternative to the penile plethysmograph (Blasingame, 1996, 2000b; Seghorn & Ball, 2000). The Abel Assessment for Sexual Interest is an assessment tool that has been available only since 1995; although, over 20,000 persons have experienced the procedure (Abel, personal communication, 2000). The procedure involves the client viewing 160 slides of potentially sensual pictures, including pictures of children, teens and adults, and several potential areas of paraphilic interests. The procedure does not involve penile measurement. Along with the computer-based portion of the AASI is a lengthy self-report questionnaire including a sexual history. Completion of the computer portion of the AASI is not done independently of the questionnaire. The two data sources combine systematically to provide significant assessment information.

Abel (1998) found high reliability and validity comparing the Abel Assessment for Sexual Interest with the penile plethysmograph. Certainly one advantage of the Abel Assessment for Sexual Interest is that no depictions of nude children or deviant acts are utilized in the procedure (Blasingame, 1996; Seghorn & Ball, 2000). Others have also found the Abel Assessment for Sexual Interest outcome comparable to the penile plethysmograph outcome data (Johnson & Listiak, 1999; Letourneau, 1999).

The AASI slide stimuli do not include full nudity or sexual activity. While viewing the slides, the clients are instructed to rate each picture in terms of being "sexy to me," "maybe sexy or sometimes sexy," or "not sexy to me" (Blasingame, 2000b). These are modified instructions for the Abel Assessment for Sexual Interest given to persons with developmental disabilities. Mainstream client instructions involve rating the slides on a scale of one through seven. The self-report rating of the respective sexual attraction or desirability of each slide is indicated when the client presses a button on a laptop computer. Colored stickers on the keys make it easier for clients to make their selection.

The client's rating of the slides tabulates by category of interest, including young children, male or female, etc. In addition to the self-report ratings provided by the client, the computer compiles objective data regarding viewing behavior and interest beyond the client's awareness (Abel, 1998). The computer measures the client's reaction for each of the twenty-two categories of potential interest with multiple slides in each category. The raw data converts to Z-scores and into a bar graph format. Because these are ipsative scores (not normative data, i.e. not comparing the client to other persons), the bar graph represents only the individual client's preferences and ratings of the slide stimuli by category. Each client demonstrates his/her understanding of the procedure and rating process during a practice tray of slides in order to rehearse their understanding of what they are to do. The evaluator is typically not in the room while the actual procedure is taking place.

As an assessment tool, the AASI is effective in ascertaining the sexual interests of clients, including possibly problematic sexual behavior targets. As with penile plethysmography, a client's AASI data is not for determination of legal facts such as guilt or innocence. The presence of deviant sexual interest or preference for children is a significant risk factor for *re-offense* (Hanson & Bussiere, 1996) and becomes a major focus of intervention for those clients.

In addition to the computer-based data on the Abel Assessment for Sexual Interest, a structured interview of the client using the AASI Questionnaire is conducted (1995). As an adjustment for the client's learning and developmental disabilities, the Adolescent Version is useful with most of the adult clients because the vocabulary is at the fifth-grade comprehension level. A questionnaire specifically designed for people with developmental disabilities is currently under development (Abel, personal communication, 2001). The questionnaire solicits information regarding the client's sexual history with several problematic sexual behaviors, measures of endorsements of cognitive distortions in several related domains, alcohol and drug history, sexual fantasy preferences, trauma and personal victimization information, crime history, and other clinical interview information.

The evaluator reads the questionnaire to each client, breaking up the sections for attention span management. This allows the evaluator to make sure the client understands the nature of the questions and to ascertain the client's level of comprehension as the testing proceeds. Such a narrative process enhances the evaluation process by allowing the evaluator to pursue a greater clarification regarding particular items of inquiry throughout the assessment.

Regardless of which tool an evaluator utilizes, measurement of sexual deviance is vital when comprehensively assessing those with problematic sexual behavior. Without use of such tools, community safety may be jeopardized by overlooking important factors related to potential targets of inappropriate behavior.

OTHER FORENSIC PROCEDURES

SEX OFFENDER TYPOLOGIES

In addition to the types of sexual behavior patterns that have been identified as mental disorders or paraphilias (APA, 1994), other ways of characterizing sexual offenders have been proposed. These are commonly referred to as typologies. However, no singular typology is accepted among the professional community who treat the sexual offender population (ATSA, 1997).

One useful typology presents the construct by categorizing offenders by characteristics of their victims and lifestyle issues in relation to risk for re-offense. Abel (1995) offered the following characterizations of risk levels related to child molestation and re-offenses.

- GROUP ONE includes offenders who victimized their own biological child, also known as the incest-only offender. These persons have the lowest re-offense rates compared to other offenders (Hanson & Bussiere, 1996).

- GROUP TWO includes offenders who victimized someone they knew closely, i.e. the victim was not of their immediate biological family, but was a stepchild, family friend, or perhaps a babysitter.

- GROUP THREE includes offenders who victimized a combination of group one and two or those who had victimized a stranger.

- GROUP FOUR includes offenders whose abuse involved stalking, predatory, yet nonviolent behaviors.

- GROUP FIVE includes offenders who were predatory, violent, used weapons, and/or had antisocial personality disorder.

In Abel's construct the amenability and likelihood of benefiting from treatment decreases as the risk level increases (Abel, 1995). Determining a classification level requires not only clinical interview but also a thorough documentation review.

Another typology schema, specifically regarding persons with developmental disabilities, is from Seghorn & Ball (2000). They point out that no singular pathway leads to sexual misconduct. They note five subtypes of offenders frequently seen in persons with developmental disabilities.

- ABUSE-REACTIVE OFFENDERS are naive and suggestible persons who are abuse victims exposed to a level of sexual awareness that they are not prepared to deal with and, subsequently, act out inappropriately.

- IMMATURE OFFENDERS are persons with developmental disabilities who receive limited sex education, a problem that may lead to unacceptable expressions of normal curiosities and urges.

- IMPULSIVE OFFENDERS are persons with developmental disabilities who have concurrent neurological deficits including generalized impulse control problems. Inadequate impulse controls may lead to acting out or sexual behavior in settings not appropriate for such behavior.

- SEXUALLY COMPULSIVE OFFENDERS use sexual conduct to remedy underlying or unrecognized issues or needs. Sexual behavior may mask other mental health problems such as depression or anxiety, isolation or boredom.

- SEXUALLY FIXATED/PEDOPHILIC OFFENDERS are offenders with developmental disabilities who find comfort in the presence of children and in sexualizing those relationships.

While there is no singular typology that includes every offender, these issues are important to consider when assessing and developing a treatment plan.

ACTUARIAL RISK CLASSIFICATION

Another approach to classifying sexual offenders is to determine the likelihood of re-offense based on actuarial data. This procedure is valid when assessing a person who is a developmentally disabled sex offender with the presence of a known sexual crime conviction. Since many developmentally disabled persons do not experience adjudication in criminal court, they may not have an officially documented history. Actuarial tools are only used with those who have such documentation.

As discussed in Chapter Four, Hanson and Bussiere (1996) completed a meta-analysis of sixty-one studies and formulated a list of potential predictors of recidivism. While no singular factor was identifiable as predicting re-offense, they did identify sixty-nine factors that are contributory to sexual recidivism among known sex offenders. Their study did, however, identify sexual deviance as the highest risk factor, operationalized as phallometrically measured sexual arousal to children, general deviant sexual preferences, and a history of prior sexual offenses. Antisocial personality disorder and/or general criminality also correlate to re-offense but to a lesser degree.

A subsequent study by Hanson (1997) simplified these multiple factors into a four-item matrix, based on the actuarial data from the Hanson & Bussiere (1996) meta-analysis. The screening tool used is the *Rapid Risk Assessment for Sex Offender Recidivism* (RRASOR). The four items are 1) officially documented prior sexual offenses, 2) age at release or current age being at or above twenty-five, 3) victim being male gender, and 4) whether there was a relationship between the offender and the victim. For this study, relationship with a victim included biological children and stepchildren.

A limitation of the RRASOR is that while it included a number of studies regarding sexual offenders with low intellectual functioning, the developmentally disabled population was not studied separately in terms of risk of re-offense. The RRASOR does an excellent job of screening sexual offenders within the general population of offenders; however, there are likely several additional factors yet unidentified regarding the impact of developmental disabilities. Nonetheless, the RRASOR is a valid screening tool for use with persons with developmental and learning disabilities (Hanson, personal communication, 2000).

Another recent advance in the development of actuarial

risk assessment procedures is the Static-99 (Hanson & Thornton, 1999). The research included two large meta-analyses of sexual offender recidivism studies, the one used in development of the RRASOR and another from England. On the Static-99, points are assigned based on the presence of several factors: prior offense convictions, age over/under 25, male gendered victims, the presence or absence of a relationship with the victim, prior non-sexual crimes, offense of immediate concern relating to nonsexual violence, having stranger victims, length and presence of marital/relational status, and the total number of prior sentencing dates. Among the mainstream population of sexual offenders, the Static-99 is a very useful screening tool when official documentation is available.

The Static-99 is slightly more accurate than the RRASOR in classifying risk categories (Hanson & Thornton, 1999). The Static-99 requires access to criminal justice documentation such as police or court records. For a variety of reasons, many persons with developmental disabilities that are referred for evaluation and treatment of sexual behavior problems have no formal criminal record. Given the paucity of such official documentation, the Static-99 risk assessment is often considered an inappropriate procedure. When such official documents are available, the Static-99 becomes another useful tool in classifying levels of risk for re-offense.

An evaluator should use great caution before considering the use of informal documentation with these actuarial tools. Some suggest that using actuarial tools in the absence of official criminal justice documentation may be acceptable, although this was not the protocol of the procedure development samples. Evaluators should be cautious in making decisions from outcomes based on documents that have not been subject to legal scrutiny and due process in the legal arena. Evaluators must recognize the weight of their opinion and how their opinions can influence restriction of civil liberties.

Psychometric & Self-Report Procedures

The DD-SORT program variously utilizes the following psychometric and self-report procedures. For clients with learning disabilities and/or developmental disabilities, the testing evaluator reads aloud to them. This allows them to ask or be asked clarifying questions, demonstrating their understanding of the items presented to them during the procedures. It is important for the evaluator to ascertain each client's ability to comprehend and participate in the evaluation procedures. Procedures such as these should be completed by persons with sufficient training, education and experience to appropriately use and interpret the results.

Each client completes a standard **Personal History** form. The client, parent or caretaker who is knowledgeable of the person may complete this. Early childhood experiences, exposure to abuse, medical history, school history, alcohol and drug history, etc., are all important pieces of information to gather in the comprehensive evaluation process.

The **Jesness Inventory** was developed specifically for the forensic population and has been standardized on adults and on youths as young as eight. Persons with at least a fourth grade reading/comprehension level can complete it independently. Some of the scales have negative co-relations with IQ as measured on standardized measurements of intelligence; although, the test was not standardized with persons with developmental disabilities.

The Jesness Inventory elicits information regarding eleven

potential personality characteristics, including social maladjustment, immaturity, asocial values, social anxiety, etc. Additionally, the Jesness Inventory indicates the presence of several personality-subtypes and provides classification of various interpersonal patterns found among forensic clients. The test manual also includes treatment indications and suggestions that are very useful in treatment planning. (The Jesness Inventory is available from Multi-Health Systems at www.mhs.com.)

On the **Sexual Habits, Obsessions, and Experiences Survey** (SHOES) (Blasingame, 1999a), clients are asked to respond with a yes/no paradigm to 52 items that explore issues such as childhood traumagenic experiences, sexual boundaries violations, compulsive sexuality or sexualized coping, internalized sexual shame, and ownership of abusive behaviors. This self-report survey aids in determining the level of sexual preoccupation and sociosexual boundary violations an individual may have and functions as an integral part of the sexual history taking process. (The SHOES, learning disabled version, is available at www.woodnbarnes.com)

On the Stanfield (1992) **LifeFacts Sexuality Education** sexual knowledge screening, clients are shown forty placards presenting depictions to elicit responses regarding items that involve basic factual information about human anatomy and functions, feminine hygiene and menstruation issues, the human reproductive process, various birth control issues, sexually transmitted diseases, and the interpersonal/social aspects of sexuality and sexual relationships. The client responds to specific questions for each placard while the evaluator rates his/her level of knowledge in each domain. The Stanfield materials also include a structured curriculum designed for the developmentally disabled population. (Stanfield materials are available at 1-800-421-6534.)

On the **Socio-Sexual Knowledge and Attitude Test (SSKAT)** (Edmonson & Wish, 1975), basic sexual knowledge and attitudes are measured. Domains include anatomy, sexual functioning, relationship issues of dating and marriage, pregnancy, and sexually transmitted diseases. The SSKAT also measures the person's attitudes regarding these categories. (The SSKAT is available at www.stoeltingco.com/tests/catalog/sskat.htm)

On the **State-Trait Anger Expression Inventory-2 (STAXI-2)**, clients respond by rating their level of anger at the time of evaluation and their typical level of anger and behavioral responses when angry or furious. This is a standardized procedure validated on mainstream persons as young as sixteen and may be useful with adult clients. The test manual also provides summary information regarding various anger-coping styles identified by the test procedure. (The STAXI-2 is available from Psychological Assessment Resources at www.par.com.)

On the **Buss-Durkee Hostility Inventory,** clients provide a true/false response to 66 items. The inventory has seven subcategories related to the expression of anger and hostility. These are negativism, resentment, indirect hostility, assault, suspicion, verbal hostility, and irritability. (The Buss-Durkee is available in *Assessing Sexual Abuse: A Resource Guide for Practitioners*, Safer Society Press. 1-802-247-3132)

On the **Bumby Cognitive Distortions Scales**, clients indicate their level of agreement or disagreement with statements that would be indicative of concern in the respective scale for molestation or rape. (The Bumby scales are available in the *Adult Sex Offender Assessment Packet*, Safer Society Press. 1-802-247-3132)

The **Abel Sexual Interest Cardsort** presents clients

with 75 sexual vignettes of varying sexual interest categories, including child sexual abuse, several paraphilias, sexual violence/rape, and adult appropriate scenarios. This protocol presents adult-oriented vignettes that are not included in the Abel Assessment for Sexual Interest questionnaire. The adolescent version of the AASI includes adolescent-oriented vignettes. Both versions include potentially pedophilic and other paraphilic vignettes. (The Abel Cardsort is available in Anna Salter's *Treating Child Sex Offenders and Victims,* 1988. Sage Publications.)

The **Parental Concern Inventory-Revised** (PCI-R; Blasingame, 2000a) is a 122-item symptom checklist regarding parental concerns over the past year. The PCI-R is typically completed by the parent, caregiver, and/or by children as young as twelve. The symptoms on the checklist represent behavioral phenomena indicative of many child and adolescent diagnostic categories listed in the *Diagnostic and Statistical Manual of Mental Disorders, fourth edition* (APA, 1994). The PCI-R is useful in formulating diagnostic impressions and takes but a few minutes for a parent or care provider to complete. (The PCI-R is available at www.woodnbarnes.com)

The **Adult Behavioral Concerns Inventory** (ABCI; Blasingame, 2000c) is a 122-item symptom checklist regarding personal/behavioral concerns over the past year. A client or caretaker completes the ABCI. The symptoms on the checklist represent behavioral phenomena indicative of many diagnostic categories listed in the *Diagnostic and Statistical Manual of Mental Disorders, fourth edition* (APA, 1994). The ABCI is useful in formulating diagnostic impressions and takes but a few minutes to complete, or it can be read to the client and used within an interview process (The ABCI is available at www.woodnbarnes.com)

The **Family Violence Inventory-Offender Version** (FVI-OV; Blasingame, 1996b) is a self-report survey of several forms of aggression and domestic abuse domains. An offender completes this version, which is useful in discerning the number of personal boundaries the individual has violated or is willing to accept responsibility for. (The FVI-OV is available at www.woodnbarnes.com)

The **Family Violence Inventory-Victim Version** (FVI-VV; Blasingame, 1997) assesses exposure to various forms of family violence. It is typically completed by a parent or other caregiver or can be completed as a self-report survey with clients as young as twelve. The Family Violence Inventory is useful in ascertaining what level of exposure the client has had to these potentially traumagenic experiences. (The FVI-VV is available at www.woodnbarnes.com)

The **Child Sexual Behavior Checklist-revised** (CSBCL-r; Cavanagh-Johnson, 1998) is a multi-item checklist that covers many areas of normal childhood sexual and behavioral development. The parent or caregiver completes the checklist, indicating the presence and frequency of the index behaviors. (The CSBCL-r is available at www.TcavJohn.com)

The **Child Sexual Behavior Inventory-third version** (CSBI-3; Friedrich, 1998) is a 38-item scale assessing a broad range of sexual behaviors among children aged two through twelve. The primary female caregiver, most typically a mother, completes the form. Founded on significant research, the CSBI offers delineation of normative sexual behaviors among children. (The CSBI is available from www.mhs.com.)

No singular tool or procedure can ascertain the volume of information needed to comprehensively assess developmentally disabled persons who have sexual behavior problems. Few assessment procedures have been developed specifically for persons with developmental disabilities. The items described in this chapter require cautious interpretation and application for persons with developmental disabilities. Some procedures may not be appropriate for testing with individual clients. All testing of this nature should be completed or supervised by a licensed clinician to ensure the veracity of the outcome data.

CHAPTER SIX

TREATMENT FOR DEVELOPMENTALLY DISABLED PERSONS WITH SEXUAL BEHAVIOR PROBLEMS

COMBINING sexuality and offender-specific treatment is considered the most effective approach to addressing sexual behavior problems, both for the mainstream population as well as for those with developmental and learning disabilities. Many challenges exist in working with any sexual offender. These are complicated further by the presence of learning disabilities, mental retardation, and inadequate socialization experiences of those with developmental disabilities.

The most widely recognized and primary treatment approach for sexual offender specific treatment is *relapse prevention* of the cognitive-behavioral therapy tradition (ATSA, 1997; Alloy et al., 1999). While it is likely that most clinicians working with the sex offender population integrate a variety of methods and techniques in their work, the emerging data imply that the cognitive-behavioral strategy of relapse prevention is the most promising approach to date (cf. Mander et al., 1996; Alloy et al.; Marques, 1999; Marques et al., 1999).

In terms of specific work with people with developmental disabilities, relapse prevention and cognitive restructuring are very useful treatment strategies for those who have committed sexual offenses (Haaven et al., 1990;

Haaven & Coleman, 2000). Others have also found cognitive-behavioral modification approaches to be most advantageous for treating those with developmental disabilities (Haring, 1989). Skills training for persons with developmental disabilities can enable self-management in lieu of external control imposition as effective treatment strategies (Gardner & Cole, 1989).

Many programs for those with developmental disabilities include cognitive-behavioral strategies addressing skills for self-regulation, monitoring and self-management (Haring, 1989; Haaven et al., 1990; Blasingame 2000b). From this paradigm, learning occurs in three stages (Marlatt & Gordon, 1985; Haring). First is the acquisition of information about social behavior and rehearsal of those behaviors in appropriate settings. Second is the self-application stage wherein the client implements the new skills independently. The third stage involves adaptation and maintenance of these skills in a variety of environments, generalizing and internalizing the skills. These, of course, are core features of the relapse prevention approach for enhancing self-control.

Relapse prevention, as a self-control model, focuses on the individual detaching the self-identity from the problem behavior itself (Marlatt & Gordon, 1985) and learning to have self-control over the behavior, preventing a re-offense (Nelson et al., 1988). For an offender to prevent recurrences of the problematic behavior(s), he must learn to make self-observations about the target behaviors then apply social learning principles to specific situations. The combination of cognitive restructuring and behavioral coping skills replace the maladaptive coping mechanisms and behaviors that led the client to offend. A person acquires sexual behavior problems through maladaptive learning processes (Marlatt & Gordon; Nelson et al.). As such, they will be most responsive to the

94

application of cognitive-behavioral and social learning principles.

Cognitive-Behavioral Theory Applied to Sexual Misconduct

Sexual aggression is an acquired or learned habit according to the cognitive-behavioral and social learning approaches (Marlatt & Gordon, 1985). In this context, sexual aggression is another of many overlearned bad habits or overindulgences (Nelson et al., 1988). Sexual behaviors are on a continuum, related to their use in adaptive functioning versus maladaptive functioning (Marlatt & Gordon).

An example of a continuum of adaptive sexual functioning might be:

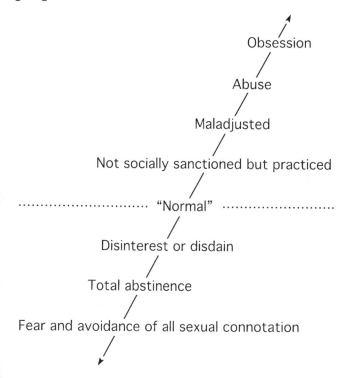

Obsession

Abuse

Maladjusted

Not socially sanctioned but practiced

·························· "Normal" ·······················

Disinterest or disdain

Total abstinence

Fear and avoidance of all sexual connotation

Faulty automatic thoughts drive maladaptive behavioral responses. Immediate gratification reinforces those responses, and is similar to other social learning processes (Marlatt & Gordon, 1985). Non-gratifying behaviors would self-extinguish and are not likely to be repeated because no reinforcement or reward for the behavior would be present.

In the cognitive-behavioral schema, deviant sexual behavior patterns are understood as complex in nature. These patterns involve situational factors, environmental factors, beliefs and expectations, personal and family histories and prior learning experiences involving aggressive behavior in all forms. These deviant sexual behavior patterns persist due to the reinforcing effects of the behavior, including familial and social reactions experienced by the aggressor before, during and after the specific aggressive sex acts or behaviors (Marlatt & Gordon, 1985; Nelson et al., 1988).

Sexually abusive behaviors are maladaptive, overlearned (thoughtless, automatic) habit patterns typically followed by immediate gratification. When done in response to stressful or unpleasant situations, they represent maladaptive coping mechanisms (Marlatt & Gordon, 1985). From this paradigm, sexual behavior patterns can change through reconditioning, cognitive restructuring, skill acquisition, and accepting responsibility for self-correction. As such, modifying sexually aggressive behavior patterns inherently involves modifying one's identity and lifestyle (Marlatt & Gordon). Beyond sexual offenses or offensive behavior, treatment foci may also include a number of independent factors that may or may not be associated with the actual offense behaviors (Marlatt & Gordon). Within this paradigm, incestuous behavior patterns include acquired relationship patterns and not only the acts of sexual or physical aggression.

RELAPSE PREVENTION & SEXUAL MISCONDUCT

Relapse prevention is a self-control program that combines several factors. These include cognitive restructuring and other cognitive interventions, behavioral skills training, lifestyle change procedures, and principles from social learning theory. Relapse prevention began in related forms of treatment in the mid to late 1970s as an application of cognitive-behavioral therapy and research (Marlatt & Gordon, 1985). Relapse prevention concepts and strategies are applicable to several disorders, including alcoholism, drug abuse, smoking, weight control, sexual behavior problems, domestic violence and impulsive aggressive behaviors. Some have described these as problems of indulgence (Nelson et al., 1988). The application of the relapse prevention model to treatment with the developmentally disabled population has been in process for some time (Haaven et al., 1990; Blasingame, 1994b; Shultz, 2000).

In brief, relapse prevention approaches include having clients learn to identify their own antecedent thoughts, feelings, and environmental factors that appear to generate higher levels of risk for repetition of the inappropriate behaviors. After the clients learn their high risk factors, they are trained in developing methods of coping more effectively with those factors through behavioral skills training (Marlatt & Gordon, 1985; Nelson et al., 1988; Bays, Freeman-Longo & Montgomery-Logan, 1990). Such interventions will likely include the concepts of avoidance of risk situations, escape from risk situations, thought stopping, and the use of support calls and other support contacts (Bays et al.). The relapse prevention approach also teaches the client ways of rebalancing his/her lifestyle, changing attitudes and beliefs, and attempting to break the pattern of negative behavior in their lives.

Each client will have his/her own cyclical pattern of dysfunctional antecedents and behaviors (cf. Nelson et al., 1988; Laws, 1989; Bays et al., 1990; Haaven et al., 1990; Ryan & Lane, 1991). This approach implies that unhealthy lifestyles and/or maladaptive, inadequate coping patterns exist in most sexual offenders. These lifestyles lead to the buildup of stress (Marlatt & Gordon, 1985; Nelson et al., 1988). As the stress builds, a person with poor coping skills and numerous cognitive distortions (Nelson et al.; Bumby, 1996) will then implement dysfunctional ways of dealing with the circumstances, increasing the likelihood of a relapse or re-offense.

Cognitive-Behavioral Therapy & Relapse Prevention Applied to Treatment with Developmentally Disabled Persons

Programs using these approaches for treatment with developmentally disabled persons have existed for some time. Examples include the Social Skills Program at Oregon State Hospital (Haaven et al., 1990) and the GAINS program developed by Hernandez and Radavsky at the Stockton Developmental Center (Shultz, 2000). Both of these are institutional programs. Community-based programs for sexual behavior problems of persons with developmental disabilities are limited in number (Shultz). Many people with developmental disabilities remain underserved.

The Developmentally Disabled Sexual Offender Rehabilitative Treatment (DD-SORT) program is a community-based program. DD-SORT offers specialized treatment services for persons with developmental and learning disabilities within a larger "mainstream" sexual offender treatment continuum of services (Blasingame, 1994b; Blasingame, 2000b). The DD-SORT program adapted the relapse prevention concepts to the developmental levels and challenges of learning among persons with developmental disabilities who also have sexual behavior problems.

PROGRAMMATIC MODIFICATIONS

The modifications to the program design and implementation adjust to the learning level of the individual client. This is known as the **zone of proximal development** in the developmental psychology literature (Vygotsky, 1978; Dacey & Travers, 1996). This construct involves identifying the actual developmental level of the individual, based on completed developmental and learning milestones, i.e. what has already been learned. This is how mental ages are commonly determined through formal psychometric procedures.

However, the individual's capabilities defined by a specific mental age do not reflect the capacity to problem solve when given supportive assistance. The difference between the person's ability to problem solve independently and his/her level of potential for problem-solving when offered guidance or collaboration with peers that are more capable, is identified as the zone of proximal development (Vygotsky, 1978).

The zone of proximal development identifies the areas of learning or developmental processes just ahead of those already learned. While this construct is applicable to the learning paths of all children, it also applies to those with developmental disabilities (Vygotsky, 1978). Use of this approach allows clinicians, teachers, parents and care providers to introduce information and experiences that will lead the person to the next level of learning and developmental accomplishment. Concrete learning limits a person with developmental disabilities (or any person) to imitative learning. On the other hand, creating a social learning environment that includes concrete and imitative learning within the zone of proximal development support empowers the client to advance to the next step of their own developmental potential (Vygotsky). The zone of proximal development reflects the difference between what one can do independently and what one can do with some help (Dacey & Travers, 1996). Certainly with guidance and tailored support, all people can learn a little more.

By design, the DD-SORT program adjusts to the needs of people designated as mildly or moderately mentally retarded. This places the mildly mentally retarded adult at a concrete cognitive functioning level consistent with the level of cognitive functioning of the pre- or early adolescent, non-abstract thinking process (Aiken, 1985). Treatment methods and content need to be continually modified to match the level of functioning of the individual, leading him/her to the next level of learning by gradually increasing the complexity of the materials and the method of learning. Generalization and assimilation of the materials through role-plays and behavior rehearsal in treatment groups, implementation and integration in the residential setting, school and/or day program environments, and community activities are an integrated process (Haaven et al., 1990; Blasingame, 2000b).

This approach requires multi-agency cooperation and collaboration (Haaven et al., 1990). The DD-SORT program works collaboratively with several regional referring agencies, multiple residential care programs, day and supported employment programs, family members, and schools. Some of the clients are on formal probation or parole, civil commitments and/or conservatorships, while others enroll on a voluntary basis. Cross training between agencies and program designs is a vital component of the collaborative efforts of each community partner involved in the delivery of services for these clients. Chapter Seven discusses these issues of community collaboration.

PROGRAM DESIGN & STRUCTURE

The SORT program (Blasingame, 1994a) uses the cognitive-behavioral and social learning theory perspectives. The philosophy views sexually inappropriate behavior as learned behavior that may be unlearned, relearned, and/ or managed. The SORT program has multiple phases/ levels of treatment. The DD-SORT program implements developmentally appropriate modifications within the cognitive-behavioral program.

PHASE ONE involves identification and ownership of the problematic sexual behavior, learning about the individuals' high risk factors and corrective interventions, and beginning to recognize the effects of the sexual misconduct on the victim.

PHASE TWO involves de-construction of the cognitive distortions and acting out cycles that enabled the inappropriate behaviors. The cognitive restructuring process is very useful with persons with developmental disabilities (Haaven et al., 1990). When appropriate, clients compose responsibility-clarifying letters to their victims or others affected by their problematic sexual behavior.

PHASE THREE involves reconstruction or re-socialization of the individual's thought process and behavioral patterns, including anger management, communication skills and emotional self-regulation. While social perspective taking, i.e. viewing one's behavior from the perspective of others, is difficult for offenders with or without learning disabilities, it is an important skill to acquire. Throughout the program an emphasis is placed on developing increased awareness of the effects of sexual abuse and/or offensive behaviors as well as on addressing the client's own victimization issues.

PHASE FOUR is a maintenance or aftercare and follow-up component with reduced session frequency and more randomized reinforcement of treatment gains.

The DD-SORT program attempts to capitalize on the application of the zone of proximal development construct in the design and implementation of therapeutic interventions. Treatment groups are open-ended, creating a treatment culture that allows new clients to enter the program and concurrently work with clients who are further along in treatment. Client-to-client interaction provides feedback and support. Group size is limited to six clients with two therapists.

In this environment, some clients may be at Phase One while others are at Phase Three. The Phase Three clients benefit from repetition and from "helping teach" the new clients, which is an application of social learning theory as well as positive programming (LaVigna, Willis, & Donnellan, 1989). This process also ensures that the materials are being presented at a level that the clients can understand, retain, and apply by allowing the clinicians to observe what life-oriented understanding the clients are "getting" or "not getting" (Marques et al., 1999; Haaven & Coleman, 2000). Application scenarios repeatedly rehearsed in treatment sessions ensure targeting the individual's zone of proximal development.

APPLICATION OF BEHAVIOR MODIFICATION PRINCIPLES

A key to treatment with developmentally disabled and/ or learning disabled persons is to match their level of vocabulary and concreteness of thinking. For many people with developmental disabilities, behavioral skill deficits are core treatment issues. Behavior therapy involves a variety of interventions, including positive programming, shaping, task analysis, chaining, prompting and fading, and generalization strategies (Handen, 1998). Positive programming of specific and detailed behaviors assists people with developmental disabilities to accomplish learning within their zone of proximal development and increases their sense of success as learners.

Shaping involves rewarding closer approximations of the desired behavior, moving in small increments. Task analysis and chaining enable treatment providers and educators to identify the singular components to larger tasks (Handen, 1998). Reinforcement for attempts of successive accomplishment of each component shapes the desired direction. Behavior chain tasks link each component to the other with reinforcement, including high fives and verbal praise, increasing the likelihood of the behaviors being paired with the sense of payoff and accomplishment (Handen). As an example of creative rewards, one of the DD-SORT therapists periodically volunteers to do push-ups in-group if the clients can recall or complete a specific program exercise. The clients try their best to give him push-ups and cheer loudly for themselves when they accomplish the deed!

Prompting and fading are concepts that are used in academic settings, athletic settings, self-help skills training, and social skills training (Handen, 1998). Prompts include physical gestures such as hand movements or postures, verbal cues, or other signals that alert the learner to attend to a specific stimuli or component of a task. Once the target behavior is paired with the prompt-stimulus and behaviors related to the task being prompted are accomplished, fading or gradual reduction of prompting allows the learner to complete tasks without dependence on the prompting (Handen). Daily life skills from hygiene to social skills increase through reinforcement. Variations and gradual reduction of prompting frequency and delayed prompting increase self-reliance. In therapy sessions, cues and prompts are used to coach clients to function in their zone of proximal development. With rehearsal, clients are able to improve their memory skills, empowering personal application of skills outside the treatment sessions.

Generalization outside the learning environment is often problematic for those with developmental disabilities (Handen, 1998). Skills need to be trained across environments and may need to involve multiple clinicians to lessen dependence on any individual as another cue of the learned behavior or skill. Training parents, care home staff, teachers, van drivers, etc., use the same prompts and reinforcers to help the person with developmental disabilities to generalize their new skills. Such generalization is vital in order for relapse prevention strategies to be effective.

Behavioral reinforcement of rehearsal and in-vivo application helps the clients integrate the concepts into their daily lives. The literature well documents the effectiveness of the use of token systems with persons with developmental disabilities (Williams, Williams & McLaughlin, 1989). While behavioral or performance demands should never prohibit access to food, privacy or other rights, using reward systems for bonus privileges or other incentives is clearly supported (Williams et al., 1989). Having the reward systems managed by the treatment program therapists rather than care home staff has allowed the DD-SORT program to achieve the benefits of behavioral rewards without sabotaging the care home staff or challenging the clients' rights within their residential or day program settings.

Baseline data for clients entering the DD-SORT program include incident reports from teachers and care providing staff, parent reports and self-report information. Based on such baseline information and other assessment outcome information, a treatment plan is implemented across environments.

TREATMENT MODALITIES

By design, the DD-SORT modalities involve individual therapy, group therapies, psycho-educational sex education and relationship skills groups. Concurrent and/or conjoint family member sessions as well as parent and caretaker support groups are useful interventions. There are frequent consultations and collaboration with the service coordinator/case manager, care home staff, schoolteachers, day program staff, job coaches, probation officers, and the clinical team. An organizational structure empowering such collaboration should be in place before treatment services begin (Haaven et al., 1990).

The DD-SORT program offers two levels of treatment groups each week; the core group focuses on sexual behavior problems and relapse prevention. A second group focuses on social relationships, sexual education, and other life skills such as anger management, communication skills, and family issues. Both groups integrate relapse prevention concepts and cognitive-behavioral intervention strategies.

The core treatment process begins with education of the basic program process and vocabulary. Clients often need to learn terms such as the appropriate names of their sexual anatomy. They also learn concepts used throughout their treatment program and in their residential and day program settings. In the initial sessions, clients learn important phrases and definitions through constant and random reinforcement.

TREATMENT TECHNIQUES & STRATEGIES

The following are techniques and strategies as adapted and used within the DD-SORT program. Residential program, day program, and job program staffs are trained to understand these concepts, allowing further application of treatment concepts within the clients' lives.

TREATMENT CREATIVITY

Learning needs to be fun (Haaven et al., 1990) as well as targeted within the zone of proximal development for each client. Many people with developmental disabilities are very creative (Coston & Lakey, 1999). Use of creative and humorous approaches includes making collages, drawing, making up songs and chants, board games, skits and role-plays. Haaven et al. suggest that the linking of emotion with the learning experience enhances learning. Creative exercises increase this connection.

Creativity also makes treatment sessions interesting when the process requires a significant amount of repetition. Treatment interventions need to be singular concepts. Progression of information building on previously learned concepts enhances learning (Brown & Pond, 1999). Visual cues, such as posters and pictures, are very helpful.

Therapist styles also need to be creative also. Modulation of voice, tone of voice, body posture and other non-verbal communication methods are attention grabbers. Therapist movement during group, i.e. moving closer to a client when it is his turn, also serves this purpose (Stacken & Shevich, 1999). Telling jokes, occasional self-depreciating humor, and being receptive to teasing by clients creates warmth, genuineness and rapport.

Therapists working with persons with developmental disabilities and sexual behavior problems need to have a good sense of humor. They also need to be willing to be genuine and sensitive to the effects of their demeanor on each client. Some clients are intimidated by eye contact. Others are easily embarrassed about sexuality, much less discussing their mistakes. Delivering therapeutic services with an empathic and respectful style and cognitive-behavioral methodology is an effective strategy (Stacken & Shevich, 1999).

Therapists working with developmentally disabled individuals need to plan to have fun. If it is fun for the therapist, it will be fun for the clients. Having therapist-client dyads perform a skit creates rapport. Having small teams competing against each other on skill building tasks improves cooperation skills and builds group cohesion.

Therapists also need to recognize that many people with developmental disabilities are skillful at acting as if they understand things when they do not (Brown & Pond, 1999). Nodding their head in the affirmative when asked if they understand is a common strategy. Therapists need to ask questions that will elicit a self-application of the concept to ascertain whether the client is able to understand a particular point. Having a client "teach" a concept to a newer client may be helpful in maintaining and reinforcing the learning process. Another strategy involves reversing roles in group sessions. This allows the client to correct the role-played mistakes of the therapist and practice healthy responses.

Therapists working with sexuality issues and clients who have developmental disabilities also need thick skin. The nature of discussing child sexual abuse, deviant sexual fantasies and behaviors, or other repugnant topics can be emotionally draining. Therapists and other professionals providing these types of services need to be creative in self-care and have healthy coping strategies to avoid burnout.

REINFORCEMENT STRATEGIES

Reinforcement of learning and behavior change makes the effort worth expending for the clients. Variation of reinforcers enables randomization and increases generalization of concepts learned. Here are a few examples of what DD-SORT staff persons use.

EMBELLISHED ATTENTION: Therapists make an extra effort to recognize and bring attention to successful learning or experimentation with behavior by group members. Exaggerated smiles, bragging for the client, high-fives, and outbursts of applause are examples of embellished attention. Verbal strokes and positive comments of respect for effort go a long way toward reinforcing efforts to learn and change.

TOKEN SYSTEMS AND BEHAVIOR CONTRACTS: Some clients prefer to receive tangible rewards for their efforts. Tokens earned for successive approximations of learning and behavior change reinforce such efforts. Client age and developmental level will dictate the types of reward goals. Tokens may be traded in for bonus items including toys for the adolescents, magazines from the counselor's waiting room, trips to the local burger stand, and various prizes from a goodie-drawer. Therapists often reward behaviors displayed at day programs, in care homes, or environments apart from the formal therapy setting, encouraging generalization across social settings.

STAFF PUSH-UPS: A perhaps not so ingenious idea involves a staff person doing ten push-ups in front of the group as a reward for the clients learning and remembering various concepts. The clients find it humorous for staff to have such a consequence.

THE FAN CLUB BOOK: Some adolescent clients enjoy the positive strokes of a Fan Club Book. Clients create a construction paper "book" in which fan club members can write comments. Fan club members usually include therapists, parents, care home staff, bus drivers, teachers, and peer group members who write positive comments about the client's behavior, character and learning efforts. Such positive reinforcement often creates aspiration to do behaviors that will gain more attention that is positive. An example of fan club book comments might be "I am Jon's fan because he is learning to control his temper!" Another might be "I like Bill because he is a caring person." Collecting entries and signatures is a great way to practice healthy assertiveness skills, a nice side effect of the project.

AVOID IT! CONTRACTS

One way to reduce the risk of a re-offense is to avoid certain situations or people. An AA member once said that if you don't want to fall, don't go to slippery places. To avoid risk situations, one must have an avoidance strategy (Bays et al., 1990). The DD-SORT application of this construct is the *Avoid It! Contract* (Blasingame, 1994b; 2000b).

Therapists review the *Avoid-It! Contract* with each client during his/her first therapy sessions. The contract explains the types of people, places and activities they are to avoid while in the treatment program. The contract is reviewed and clearly established as the rules they are expected to follow. Contract items for avoidance include sexual thinking about young children, being around children or places where children loiter, babysitting, or using pornography or alcohol. The contract format makes concrete the self-restrictions and self-prohibitions that persons might define for themselves in the course of a treatment program (Bays et al., 1990). Because many mildly developmentally disabled clients do or will eventually live in the community, acquiring these avoidance strategies are important.

The *Avoid It! Contract* encourages the client to develop self-monitoring skills that are vital if s/he is going to achieve self-management and self-control (Gardner & Cole, 1989). By requiring the clients to complete a *Weekly Check-In* form or have one read to them with assistance in completing the form within individual therapy sessions, there is increased accountability for tracking their own thoughts, fantasies, and various behaviors. These do not entail detailed fantasy logs that are nonproductive with people with developmental disabilities due to difficulties with the actual logging of details and/or risky arousal issues (Haaven et al., 1990). Self-monitoring influences positive changes in the frequencies of targeted behaviors (Gardner & Cole, 1989).

For clients who live in residential care, their avoidance of risky situations is externally controlled. Nonetheless, clients frequently report sexualized thinking about children as being stimulated by watching television programs, going on outings in the community, etc. Regular accountability for masturbatory fantasies, masturbatory frequency and location, and confrontation of deviant thinking occurs through the weekly check-in inquiry during individual therapy sessions.

THOUGHT-STOPPING

Sexual offenders in general are assumed to have a high frequency of deviant sexual thoughts and urges. When offenders who have deviant fantasies act on those thoughts, a crime is likely to result. If those arousing thoughts are changed or corrected, the person is less likely to act out in deviant ways. There is particular concern regarding offenders whose sexual interests or arousal patterns are elevated on the assessment tools, i.e. the penile plethysmograph or the Abel Assessment for Sexual Interest (discussed in chapter five). Since objectively measured deviant sexual interest in children is the most powerful risk classification indicator (Hanson & Bussiere, 1996), it is imperative to attempt to decrease the client's arousal to those themes.

Within the DD-SORT program, deviant arousal reduction efforts are focused primarily on cognitive strategies. The clients learn thought-stopping (Bays et al., 1990), using the phrase *Stop That!* Clients are required to report if they have "bad, nasty thoughts," specifically regarding sexual thinking involving children, exhibitionism, public masturbation, or other conduct for which they have gotten into trouble. Clients learn that many sexual thoughts are "good sexy" thoughts as well. Concrete labeling of thoughts and behaviors (Monat, 1982; Haaven et al., 1990) with explanation to each client ensures comprehension of the vocabulary used. Age appropriate and healthy sexual fantasies are also discussed, described, and encouraged in therapy sessions.

Another thought management exercise involves a worksheet entitled *Stop That, Think Different, and Act Better*. This cognitive skill exercise enables clients to think before they act. (This worksheet is in the program forms manual accompanying this book.)

Yet another component of the thought-stopping and/or thought management process involves covert sensitization strategies. These include teaching the clients to pair an uncomfortable consequence when they experience deviant fantasies (bad, nasty thoughts) or a pleasurable consequence when they experience healthy fantasies (good, sexy thoughts). As an example, we may ask a client to think about telling his probation officer about his thoughts of sexually touching a child at the park. Or perhaps the client will be asked to role play how a father may treat him when it is discovered that the client has molested a child. On the other hand, the client can be asked to think about how good it feels when having good sexy thoughts about his age-appropriate, consenting partner.

Arousal control techniques that are more behaviorally oriented include odor aversion, verbal satiation, and masturbatory satiation techniques. Not all mainstream offender treatment programs utilize these techniques, and many working with the developmentally disabled population are disinclined to use these techniques due to their aversive and/or intrusive nature. These methods do not increase normal arousal patterns. Some have advocated that such a direct or overt focus on deviant arousal reduction is not necessary when other interventions are in place (Marshall, 1999).

DANGER ZONES AKA HIGH RISK FACTORS

Certain social contexts, situations, or factors need to be in place for a sexual re-offense to occur. Such high-risk situations may include the presence of certain emotional states, the presence of a potential victim and/or being under the influence of alcohol, drugs or similar disinhibitors (Nelson et al., 1988). Risk situations involve loosing control over abstinence from the inappropriate behavior, in this case, sexual misconduct (Bays & Freeman-Longo, 1989). Risk factors may be internal, external, or a combination of the two (Marlatt & Gordon, 1985).

A major treatment and supervision concept is that of the "Danger Zone." A danger zone is "a place where I could get hurt or I could hurt someone else." In the initial sessions, clients memorize the phrase and definition. Clients learn to identify their own danger zones in a concrete fashion at the beginning of their program by completing a worksheet entitled *Identifying Danger Zones* (Blasingame, 1994b; 2000b). The worksheet identifies examples of internal danger zones including feelings, thoughts, and behavioral triggers as well as external danger zones that include locations and types of people that may trigger making wrong sexual choices. Another danger zone worksheet entitled *My Danger Zones* assists clients in applying the concept even more personally.

Over time, clients learn to reconsider their life situations using cognitive restructuring and personalizing their understanding of danger zones. The concrete and instructional methods give them a starting point. Along with identifying high-risk situations or factors, clients also learn "Smart Talk," self-instructional statements useful in cognitive restructuring and self-management (Haaven et al., 1990; Gardner & Cole, 1989). "Smart Talk" (self-instructive statements) includes directives to stop a thought or behavior, self-redirections to alter thoughts or behaviors or to "Leave It!" (escape a situation). They also include self-reinforcement or self-praises such as "good job!" when they escape the danger zones.

Clients are encouraged to evaluate the outcomes of their choices, including their "Smart Talk." Self-consequenting (Gardner & Cole, 1989) is sometimes used by clients who apply their own aversive consequences by snapping their wrist with a rubber band when they experience a deviant or "bad nasty" thought. Aversive techniques are not imposed on clients in the DD-SORT program and are only implemented by the client. Nonetheless, for clients who are so motivated, aversive wrist snapping or making corrective self-comments serves the self-management purpose well.

Many clients discuss their danger zones with their care home and job program staff. This serves to elicit their reinforcement, to assist in avoiding certain situations, and to provide redirection and positive programming to support the client as s/he learns to exert greater self-control. The relapse prevention approach includes developing a support system to assist in monitoring and encouraging working one's program.

SAFE PLANS

Each client needs a "Safe Plan" (Blasingame, 2000b) using these self-management and intervention strategies. The "Safe Plan" concept encompasses the relapse prevention constructs of corrective intervention, self-confrontation and self-management. It also defines internal and external boundaries within which the client will function. Safe plans include training self-talk scripts (Haaven et al., 1990; Bays et al., 1990) such as "stay away from kids," avoidance and escape strategies, and rehearsal of how to "get help!" by "using my words." (Complete instructions on how to develop a "Safe Plan" are in the accompanying program forms book.)

"Safe Plan" trainings for care home, day program, job program, and chaperoning family members focus on external management. It includes where the client can go or not go, types of movies or stimuli that may be dangerous influences for the client, and the level of line-of-sight supervision and management needed to ensure community safety. Day and residential program staff and caretakers are taught to redirect those who are found to leer and gawk at children, attempt to approach or touch children, or are verbally or physically inappropriate toward non-consenting individuals.

SELF-MANAGING WITH SCRIPTED SELF-TALK

Clients learn several cognitive self-management concepts through training in scripted self-talk statements. Self-talk has significant influence on human behavior and self-esteem (Bays et al., 1990). Integrating self-talk within the self-management and self-control paradigm, the DD-SORT program developed "The Big Five."

They are as follows:
1) I can control my choices and my behavior.
2) I can say no to wrong sex behavior.
3) I am the boss of my own body, only.
4) I follow the "Private Parts Rules."
5) I can stay away from danger and off the *Ladder to Trouble* (discussed below).

The "Private Parts Rules" involve the scripting of:
1) If it has to do with *private parts*, then;
2) It is to be done at a *private time*,
3) In a *private place*,
4) If it involves someone else, I need *permission or consent*.

Clients learn the distinction between private and public behaviors. Private means "only for me," and public means "others can see" or "outside my bedroom or bathroom."

Clients learn "The Big Five" concepts and other adaptations of relapse prevention skills throughout the program by using rote memorization, games, and memory contests to reinforce learning and application. Additionally, clients learn to integrate these self-management concepts via role-play and other group activities within sessions.

OFFENSE PATTERN IDENTIFICATION

Several models of cycles or offense chains exist (Bays & Freeman-Longo, 1989; Ryan & Lane, 1991; Haaven & Coleman, 2000) following the cognitive-behavioral model of re-offense (Nelson et al., 1988). Inherent to the construct are the notions that maladaptive coping and inadequate problem-solving lead to stress buildup and are cyclical in nature. Use of maladaptive coping strategies and cognitive distortions acquired through classical conditioning, conditioned compensatory responses, and reinforcement of the behaviors facilitates repetition of the deviant or inappropriate behaviors (Marlatt & Gordon, 1985). In terms of sexually deviant behaviors, certain risk factors may be more important to certain individuals, making it impossible to delineate a one-size-fits-all profile. However, as noted above regarding "Danger

Zones," clients learn to identify individual internal and external risk factors or situations that heighten their risk for re-offense.

Several deficits interfere with the functioning of those with developmental disabilities (Seghorn & Ball, 2000). These include cognitive distortions or thinking errors, empathy deficits, inadequate sexual knowledge or training, inadequate communication skills, anger management problems, deviant sexual development, lack of self-awareness, and deviant arousal patterns. Each of these problem areas may well contribute to the person's cycle of dysfunctional or maladaptive behaviors.

As the client becomes able to memorize concepts by rote, the concept of the "Ladder to Trouble" or "The Ladder" for short (Blasingame 1994b; 2000b), a version of the assault cycle (Nelson et al., 1988; Bays & Freeman-Longo, 1989; Ryan & Lane, 1991), is introduced to the client. A poster-sized chart permanently displays "The Ladder" in the group room. The phases of learning to use this tool involve the rote memorization of the names of the steps on the ladder, then the definition of the concepts represented by each step on the ladder, and finally, learning personal "Safe Plan" interventions to prevent relapse or re-offense. ("The Ladder" model is included in the program forms manual.)

The seven steps on the ladder are labeled with the following phrases, from the bottom up. (See diagram on page 118.)

STEP ONE involves feeling bad about a problem or situation. Negative affective states, boredom and anger are often used as examples.

STEP TWO involves poor problem-solving or coping

skills that result in keeping the emotions and issues of step one to oneself.

STEP THREE on the ladder involves sexualizing the solutions to one's problems and/or using deviant sexual fantasies. The ladder construct has been adapted by labeling step three as "angry" thoughts instead of sexual thoughts for those with anger problems.

#7 Act Out/Bad Behavior
#6 Set Up/Opportunity
#5 Danger Zones
#4 (Bad) Nasty Thoughts
#3 Wrong Way Thinking
#2 Keep Things to Myself
#1 Feel Bad

STEP FOUR involves use of cognitive distortions or thinking errors that justify proceeding toward the deviant acts or bad behavior. (Wrong way thinking is discussed on the following page.)

STEP FIVE involves being in an actual "Danger Zone" or high-risk situation. Many clients identify that their danger zones are combinations of steps one through four.

STEP SIX involves either purposely setting up a situation in which to act out, or taking advantage of opportunities that seemingly present themselves to the offender.

STEP SEVEN indicates that the actual deviant acts are committed.

At their own pace, the clients begin to develop their own application of each step on the ladder, using a worksheet entitled *My Ladder*. This process is similar to mainstream protocols involving cycle work and is a primary relapse prevention intervention (Bays & Freeman-Longo, 1989). Individual sessions tutor and assist the clients in exploring their own history, identifying their own pattern, and devising intervention, aka "Safe Plan," strategies for self-control and self-management.

IDENTIFYING COGNITIVE DISTORTIONS & SELF-CORRECTION

Another major treatment concept is that of cognitive distortions or thinking errors (Yochelson & Samenow, 1977; Haaven et al., 1990). Thinking errors enable all of us to do behaviors that we know are wrong and/or socially unacceptable. Faulty thinking, negative self-talk, negative affective states, and perception and misperception influence behavioral decision making and coping responses (Nelson et al., 1988; Bays & Freeman-Longo, 1989). It is cognitive distortions, or thinking errors, that drive an offender's cycle (Bays & Freeman-Longo; Ryan & Lane, 1991).

The DD-SORT program uses "Wrong Way Thinking" a modified version of Haaven et al.'s (1990) conceptualizations of the cognitive distortions, referred to as criminal self-talk. These simplified labels for the thinking errors enable the clients to memorize and apply the thinking error concepts. In-group activities, role-plays, and games allow the clients to learn to identify and challenge each other when using wrong way thinking. Concrete language is used, as well as phrasing that is developmentally appropriate, to teach the clients to identify and confront their thinking errors.

Examples of wrong way thinking include "liar-liar," "sexy to me," "she wanted it," "don't go there," "wasn't me," and "not a big deal." (The entire list is included in the accompanying program forms book.) DD-SORT clients have been instrumental in labeling these concepts over time.

To ensure the clients are learning to confront their own wrong way thinking, one strategy involves soliciting examples of each thinking error. The therapist writes them on a marker board, each group member can contribute. After the board fills with examples, the therapists reads each one aloud asking who has had that thought. As clients raise their hand, they are to describe the thoughts, feelings and behaviors associated with that wrong way thinking. Another strategy involves having clients tell about when they made "that mistake."

While learning about their wrong way thinking, clients also learn "Smart Talk" self-instructional statements useful in cognitive restructuring and self-management (Haaven et al., 1990; Gardner & Cole, 1989). "Smart Talk" responses are written on 3x5 or 5x7 cards to be carried or posted on a bulletin board. Again, these self-instructive statements include directives, for example, to stop a thought or behavior, "Stop That!," self-redirections to alter thoughts or behaviors or to "Leave It!" or "Escape!" a situation, as well as to self-reinforce or self-praise saying "good job!" Collages are also creative strategies through which clients can identify situations that would be "Danger Zones," "Wrong Way Thinking," or good use of "Smart Talk."

AFFECTIVE REGULATION SKILLS

Affective self-regulation is a difficult task for many sexual offenders. Inadequate impulse control skills interfere with gaining self-control of sexual behavior problems. Problematic coping with emotions may impair an individual's ability to make healthy choices (Brown & Pond, 1999). Keeping oneself from being overly aroused emotionally empowers better cognitive processing.

Cognitive-behavioral strategies including self-monitoring of emotions are useful in this area. Clients learn to use relaxation exercises and deep breathing skills. It is important for people with developmental disabilities learn to identify and express their emotions. Learning to cope with emotional distress without reactive behavior reduces impulsivity and aggression problems. Skits and role-plays help clients learn to differentiate thoughts, feelings and behavior through behavior rehearsal.

Sexuality Education & Social Skills

Many people with developmental disabilities have had inadequate learning opportunities regarding sociosexual behaviors. Many clients with developmental disabilities are lacking in knowledge of the basic skills of autoerotic self-stimulation. Others may experience significant frustration from their incomplete or ineffective masturbatory efforts toward orgasm. Some may need training in methods to overcome this skill deficit. DD-SORT therapists accomplish such training via the training videotapes for males with developmental disabilities, *Hand Made Love,* and *Under Cover Dick* (Hingsberger, 1995 & 1996). *Finger Tips* is also available for females with developmental disabilities (Hingsberger & Haar, 2000).

Therapists using such materials with people with developmental disabilities need to discuss the content of the materials with the client and/or appropriate adult care providers or conservators before performing such procedures. It would be prudent to document such conversation or obtain written consent from a parent or conservator. Periodically, it may be necessary to allow the client to use such a tape in the privacy of his/her own room or home.

Some clients also lack basic personal hygiene and social skills. These too can be taught, as needed, in individual sessions. Training videotapes for several skills are available from Stanfield or other commercial sources. As with most packaged products, the clinician working with the developmentally disabled person will need to be prepared to work with the materials and ensure they are developmentally adapted to the client's actual zone of proximal development.

The adjunct "life skills" treatment group of the DD-SORT treatment program involves training for sexual education, social skills and relationships training. The curriculum includes the Stanfield *LifeFacts* materials and the Stanfield *Circles* video-based series regarding relationships. Therapists need to use these materials by viewing the videotape content with the clients, then processing the content through in-group discussion. Sexuality training involves not only teaching about body parts and biological functions but also the integration of healthy sexual and social boundaries, personal rights, personal choices and integrity, and consenting relationships as a greater context in which human sexuality occurs.

The life skills group also includes training regarding sexually transmitted diseases, condom use, and issues of consent. Condom training includes having the clients practice placing a condom on a rubber model of a penis. This approach leads to better assimilation of the sexual knowledge of base materials and allows for the blending of relapse prevention concepts as well. DD-SORT therapists give condoms to adolescent and adult clients to take home at their request.

> Here is a humorous example of concrete learning and the need to be realistic about sexual education. A female therapist was leading a sex education group for women with developmental disabilities. The therapist brought in a cucumber and a box of condoms. She had the women practice putting the condom on the cucumber, stating that the cucumber is taking the place of a man's penis. Two weeks later, one of the women came to group excited about having had sex with a boyfriend. The therapist asked if she had used a condom. The woman replied, "No, I didn't have one of those green things to put it on."

Clients learn additional personal growth skills including anger management, boundaries, assertiveness, communication, emotional self-regulation, relaxation techniques, consent clarification skills, differentiation of ages, and age appropriate targets of sexual attraction. Other skills include problem-solving, conflict resolution, and developing frustration tolerance. Teaching models for many of these subjects and skills have been developed such as those available from Stanfield or other resources (Antonello, 1996). The DD-SORT program modifies these commercial resources to integrate with the relapse prevention concepts noted above to make them personally applicable for the clients as well as to maintain program integrity.

Sex education efforts need to consider the environment the client lives in. At times, the interventions will challenge systemic issues and may be distressing to those involved in arriving at a solution. Nonetheless, when the problematic sexual behavior has a genesis in the care home structure, it may have to be the staff that makes changes rather than the client. For example, if the parents of a teenager complain that when they enter his room they find him masturbating, perhaps the parents need to learn to knock first. Care home staff, likewise, need to respect the privacy of those living there.

REFERRAL FOR MEDICATION MANAGEMENT

Psychopharmacological intervention is often necessary with individuals with developmental disabilities who have behavioral and impulse control problems (Handen, 1998). Those with obsessive sexual thinking, compulsive or ritualized behaviors, self-injurious behaviors, mental health problems such as attention deficit hyperactivity disorder, depression, anxiety disorders, or psychotic disorders may benefit from a formal psychiatric evaluation for medication. Non-physicians are encouraged to refer and collaborate with treating physicians and psychiatrists when treating sexual offenders who have developmental disabilities.

There are two primary paths of pharmacological intervention for sexual offenders (Sherak, 2000). First is the area of sexual hormone reduction. Second is an area that is less sexually specific, addressing co-morbid mental health problems that may exacerbate the person's difficulties with deviant sexual thinking or urges. The following is a brief overview of the classes and uses of various medications typically used with children and adults who have developmental disabilities. Not all persons with developmental disabilities or sex offense histories need medication, and this information does not substitute for consultation with a physician.

Hormonal treatment involves prescription of anti-androgenergic medication (Land, 1995; Bradford, 1997; Sherak, 2000). There are significant side effects of concern. Medications such as medroxyprogesterone (MPA) and cyproterone acetate (CPA) reduce the sexual drive by reducing the males' testosterone level (Land). Subsequently, there is a significant lowering of the deviant fantasies and arousal patterns (Sherak). One medical treatment goal is to reduce the male's level of testosterone to that of preadolescence thus reducing the sexual drive. Unfortunately, there is little research specific to men with developmental disabilities using anti-androgens; although, these medications are common in the treatment of various paraphilias.

MPA and CPA function to reduce testosterone levels. Common side effects include osteoporosis, hot and cold flashes, thrombophlebitis, muscle cramps, transient impotence, diabetes mellitus, nightmares, and gall stones

(Sherak, 2000). These are significant side effects. Staff working with people with developmental disabilities receiving MPA must be aware of these potential side effects. MPA has a positive effect on reducing recidivism of sexual offense (Bradford, 1997; Sherak). Anti-androgenergic medication usage for this purpose functions as a form of chemical castration (Bradford).

Those with attention-deficit hyperactivity disorder often take stimulant medications. This disorder effects between 9% and 18% of children with mental retardation (Handen, 1998). There is a 62% to 70% positive response for persons with mild to moderate levels of developmental disabilities taking such medications (Handen). Youth with attention-deficit hyperactivity disorder are prone to other disruptive behavior disorders, including oppositional defiant disorder and conduct disorder (Fava, 2000). Also related to these conditions are irritability, aggressiveness, outbursts of anger, and significant impulse control problems. Common stimulant medications include methylphenidate (Ritalin) and dextroamphetamine (Handen; Fava). Persons with developmental disabilities may be prone to a higher number of side effects of such medications (Handen). Monitoring for motor tics and social withdrawal needs to be attended to by parents or care home staff. Managing impulse control disorders such as attention-deficit hyperactivity disorder is important for those who also have sexual behavior problems.

A number of persons with developmental disabilities receive neuroleptic medications, commonly known as anti-psychotic medications. Handen (1998) reported that approximately 30% of institutionalized persons with mental retardation received neuroleptics. These medications are useful in the treatment of aggressive behavior, hyperactivity, self-injurious behavior, stereotyped behaviors, and antisocial behaviors (Handen). Trade names for this class of medications are Haldol, Mellaril, Thorazine, Resperidol, and Clozapine. A major side effect of these types of medications is tardive dyskinesia (Fava, 2000), a neuromuscular weakening that can potentially cause permanent nerve damage. Neuroleptic medications target aggressiveness in general, not sexual deviance. There is also evidence that neuroleptic medications dull the cognitive capacities of those who take them, a side effect even more problematic for those with developmental disabilities (Sherak, 2000).

Persons with developmental disabilities with seizure control and behavioral concerns often receive anticonvulsant medications (Handen, 1998). Handen reports that between 12% and 16% of children with moderate mental retardation and about 6.6% of children with mild mental retardation are prescribed anticonvulsant medications. There is some evidence that anticonvulsant medications interfere with learning, cognition and motor functioning.

Less than 2% of adults and children with mental retardation receive antidepressant medications (Handen, 1998). Selective serotonin reuptake inhibitors (SSRIs) relieve depression, compulsiveness and aggressive behavior (Sherak, 2000). A well-known side effect of the SSRI medications is that of reduced sexual drive and deviant fantasies (Sherak). Their use for work with paraphilics is promising (Bradford, 1997). SSRI medications are common in the treatment of sexual offenders and others with sexual compulsions or paraphilic behavior problems (Land, 1995).

Physicians and psychiatrists working with developmentally disabled persons who have sexual behavior problems will need to be judicious when assessing and monitoring for potential side effects. The research relating some of these drugs to those with developmental disabilities is sparse. While antiandrogrens have the greatest effect on sexual misconduct, the potential side effects of those medications will need a high level of staff and physician monitoring (Sherak, 2000).

Most clinicians and psychiatrists working with people with developmental disabilities agree that treatment planning and delivery of services works best when done in a multidisciplinary approach. Overall, effectiveness of therapeutic efforts and medications improve when administered in a collaborative and integrated fashion.

MORE TREATMENT STRATEGIES

Numerous other treatment strategies are useful in therapy with persons with developmental disabilities. These include family therapy, leisure and community skills, self-help and adaptive skills, and parenting skills. Implementation and application of these strategies of a more generic therapy approach are useful tools for empowering clients who have developmental disabilities. Using a cognitive-behavioral framework from which to build allows clinicians to integrate these other methods and enables client specific treatment to be implemented.

CHAPTER SEVEN ══

BUILDING COMMUNITY PARTNERSHIP & POLICIES FOR PROVIDING TREATMENT SERVICES, RESIDENTIAL CARE, SERVICE COORDINATION & PROBATION MONITORING

MANY sexual offenders live in any given community. Members of the community at large often have fears about these sexual offenders and some have a "not in my back yard" mentality. Nonetheless, sexual offenders, with and without disabilities, do live and will continue to live in the community. Community safety is a very important consideration (ATSA, 1997). In the interest of promoting community safety, collaboration between agencies and providers needs to be maximized. The following concepts are offered to further this goal.

COMMUNITY PARTNERSHIP & COMMUNICATION

Community partnership and collaboration is vital in forming and maintaining community-based treatment programs. Capitalizing on community resources, developing additional resources, and networking requires active communication between each of the providers, programs and service agencies working with the developmentally disabled person. Community partners can include the regional case management agency, residential care providers, day and job program providers, participating psychiatrists, probation officers and parole agents, client rights advocates, classroom teachers, behavior management consultants, parents/family members, as well as sexual offender treatment program clinical service providers.

Developing communication systems between agencies requires a conscientious effort to effectively share and/or manage information that is highly personal and private. Persons with developmental disabilities are entitled to all the rights and privileges of confidentiality. Their information should be protected from others who do not have their permission to know and/or a need to know. It is important to assist persons with developmental disabilities by thoroughly explaining the degree and limitations of any authorization or release forms.

There are three types of information that community partners need consent to share: private information, confidential information, and privileged communication.

- Private information is that which a person would only share with an intimate person in their life, such as a parent, partner or close friend. Team members are obligated to allow clients to choose with whom, and to what degree, private information may be shared (Huber & Baruth, 1987).

- Confidentiality has to do with professional ethics related to information shared in therapy sessions or information that exists in the person's file. Confidentiality allows the client to share with their therapist, psychiatrist, service coordinator, or other service provider extremely sensitive information such as that revealed in the process of the evaluation related to their sexual offense history, personal sexual habits, and other similar health information. Confidentiality is a concept established in the professional licensing codes and professional member organizations' codes of ethics (Huber & Baruth, 1987). Maintaining confidentiality allows the client to divulge highly sensitive information and solicit professional assistance without the concern of being stigmatized or discriminated against due to the disclosure of a repugnant behavior. This may be especially important when it involves people who have committed acts of sexual misconduct or deviance.

- Privileged communication is related to that which may or may not be shared in an open court (Huber & Baruth, 1987), particularly against a person's will. All clients have the civil right to have their communications with a therapist safeguarded from government intrusion. Only by the client's own consent or a court order should such information be shared from the witness stand. In the case of persons with developmental disabilities, there may also be a conservator appointed to be involved in making such legal decisions.

Formal release forms are necessary for establishing a record of consent for communication of an otherwise confidential and privileged nature. The form should list each person and/or agency as well as the specific types of information authorized for release between the team members.

Limitations of privacy, confidentiality and privileged communication should be discussed with each client or their conservator at the outset of intervention. As a signature on a form is easy to obtain, ethical considerations need to be implemented to ensure the person with developmental disabilities has a reasonable understanding of who will know what about them, and that they have the legal right to withdraw their consent. Obviously there are situations when this right may be restricted such as

131

when the client has been civilly committed and/or is otherwise ordered by a court to comply with specific requirements.

A further ethical consideration for team members is to be sure the client has sufficient understanding of what treatment services, residential living expectations and case management expectations will entail. Informed consent is a concept embedded in professional organizations' codes of ethics, and is legislated in some states.

Clients should also be directly told what disclosures will not be held in confidence. This would involve mandatory child abuse, dependent adult abuse, and/or elder abuse laws, as well as danger to self or others regulations, and issues related to compliance with court or similar legal requirements.

By constructing a team communication system, the client can know that the members of the team are working together. To reduce triangulation, team members forewarn clients that secrets will not be kept. Therapeutic contracts may be beneficial in assisting clients to know what is expected of them and the nature of the team communication process.

A team such as this, referred to as a sex offender treatment team, should have at least monthly meetings. While protecting necessary confidential information, communication between team members can focus on current problems encountered by or with individual clients. Team meetings are also the most appropriate setting to establish policies and protocols regarding the issues faced by the various team members. By participation in such meetings, all parties involved increase their knowledge and skills related to this unique type of clientele and program (Haaven et al., 1990).

IDENTIFYING ROLES & DEVELOPING COLLABORATION

In the mainstream sexual offender treatment community, a particularly effective community management model has evolved, commonly referred to as the "containment model" (English et al., 1996; English, 1998). In this model, a community-based team holds the offender accountable through multidisciplinary collaboration focused on maintaining community safety while allowing sexual offenders to live in the community. Part of the construct of containment involves case management and supervision of the person's activities in the community, adherence to treatment and probation/parole requirements, and a high level of accountability. In the mainstream sexual offender programs, the client is in the center of a triangle of the treatment program, the probation officer or parole agent, and a polygraph examination. The Sexual Offender Rehabilitative Treatment (SORT) program, which is the parent program of the DD-SORT program described in Chapter Six, is based on the containment model.

However, as discussed earlier, polygraph testing is not an empirically valid tool to use with persons who have developmental disabilities (Blasingame, 1998). In the case of those with developmental disabilities, the third member of the triangle is likely to be a caretaker or residential care provider who monitors and supervises the client's coming and going within the community. In addition, if the client is not on probation, the service coordinator or case manager may fill that role of accountability to the individual services plan by addressing any sexual behavior problem issues.

Identifying roles of collaborating team members is important in order to avoid confusion and conflict. Planning the process of cross-agency information management and role implementation strategies are defined in the form of an official written protocol, with a mission statement and confidentiality policy statement established before starting services. In most situations, the regional case management agencies for those with developmental disabilities will need to take the lead in forming such a team. While others, such as probation or parole divisions, could provide the leadership needed, it is best done by an agency commissioned to work with/for those with developmental disabilities in order to have the focus of specialized care for those with developmental disabilities. Also, not all persons with developmental disabilities who have sexual behavior problems will be on probation or parole. Regional case management agencies for the developmentally disabled are also able to bring together several community players whom others may have more difficulty accessing, including client rights advocates and attorneys specializing in issues related to the developmentally disabled.

Cross-training between community partner agencies is one way to increase effectiveness of the collaborative effort. As an example, social workers or service coordinators and care home staff will need additional training to understand the nature of relapse prevention and sexual offender specific treatment. On the other hand, therapists will need additional training regarding the role of the service coordinator, client rights advocate, and residential care program staff. Care home staff will need additional training to understand the technicalities of a client's probation terms and personal danger zones. Probation officers need additional training specific to increasing their understanding of people with developmental disabilities.

One of the benefits of the collaborative partnership is that the responsibility of community safety and supervision becomes a shared responsibility. Another benefit is that increased integration of the relapse prevention concepts can occur across settings and the milieu environment. This is consistent with the literature supporting positive programming for persons with developmental disabilities (LaVigna et al., 1989). In these environments, the collaborative efforts enhance the social learning process.

Most of the roles of the various community partners will be easily defined. These include:

- Service coordinators, who represent the regional referring agency, will function as case managers and fill a key role as the ultimate conduit for information flow.

- Residential care program administrators and staff are responsible for the day-to-day care and activities of each client.

- Day program and job coaches are responsible for the structuring of daily activities, practical skills development and enhancing social skills in various opportune situations.

- Treatment providers are responsible for assessing, diagnosing and treating mental health as well as sexual offense issues of each client and often serve as consultants to the various residential and day programs.

- Probation officers and parole agents play a key role by supporting the clients who are enrolled in such programs and holding the clients responsible and accountable for compliance with court orders or other legal obligations.

Community Management of Persons with Developmental Disabilities who have Sexual Behavior Problems

For people with developmental disabilities who are in residential care, day programs and/or sheltered workshops or industry programs, there are several additional benefits to this collaborative team approach. Specialized job programs for those with developmental disabilities and/or care homes that have only residents who have sexual misconduct problems or offense histories can provide unique programmatic advantages.

Some of those advantages include consistent program rules related to sexual misconduct risk management, Safe Plan implementation, and increased consistency in managing in-program activities such as community outings and supervision of potential contact with children or other vulnerable persons by the offender. Specialized homes and programs are also more likely to be consistent in supporting probation or other legal requirements. Staff familiarity and consistency are important considerations when discussing community management of sexual offenders who have developmental disabilities.

> Case Example: A developmentally disabled client, a young adult pedophile with multiple male and female victims, was living in a low-level non-specialized care home. The staff was not trained to watch for risk signs or "Danger Zones." The staff did not like the pressure from the treatment program to monitor the client's coming and going in the community. In fact, they argued with the client and program regarding how dangerous the client was and felt that he should not be restricted or in line-of-sight supervision. Week after week, the staff sent him to his treatment group

on a public bus. The client reported weekly having fantasies on the bus about sexual touching of the children he sat next to. He reported masturbatory fantasies about those children. The program was eventually successful in convincing the referring agency and client that the bus ride was a danger zone to be avoided. The client agreed to transfer to a higher level of care at the next opening. The care home staff persisted in their position that he was not a danger to the community.

In the milieu of each setting, clients are encouraged to increase responsibility for themselves and to develop ownership of personal choices and behaviors. In homes and programs that specialize in care and services for persons with developmental disabilities who have sexual behavior problems, a more consistent and systematic environment is implemented. Care homes with poorly trained staff members or homes that have a mixed residential population of offenders and non-offenders may find the required restrictions imposing or difficult to consistently follow. Care homes serving the sexual offender population will require staff to have specialized training. Sexual offenders with developmental disabilities who live in community homes and programs in lieu of prison or other institutions need to be recognized for the danger they represent to the community.

Many persons with developmental disabilities who have sexual behavior problems are very impulsive and distractible. As such, they may represent a heightened risk to children or other vulnerable adults in their environment. In the past, persons who were so impulsive may well have been placed in an institution, but that is no longer the case. The current trend involves less restrictive environments and more community-based services for these clients.

Line-of-sight supervision may be required for many sexual offenders who have developmental disabilities (Blasingame, 2000b). In the mainstream sexual offender treatment programs, there is a prohibition against offenders being alone with minors at any time while on probation or in the treatment program (Blasingame, 1994a). This restriction is also a common term of probation or parole, focusing on community safety. The line-of-sight restriction is clearly appropriate for clients who are diagnosed with pedophilia, frottage, or other similar paraphilias.

Job programs - or sheltered workshops or industries that specialize in work with developmentally disabled sexual offenders - are able to identify jobs and projects that can keep the potential danger to the community minimal. With higher staff-to-worker ratios, line-of-sight supervision, and discrete job assignments, the clients are exposed to fewer "Danger Zones" and are encouraged to follow their "Safe Plans." In these cases, ongoing modeling and behavioral rehearsal of "Safe Plans" implementation increase the likelihood of generalization and internalization by the clients.

Residential care programs that specialize in work with developmentally disabled sexual offenders are better able to manage decisions about community activities and outings. Certainly, sex offenders should avoid places where they would have heightened exposure to the "Danger Zones" or high risk factors, including trips to children's parks, places where youth loiter without adult supervision, etc. As the residential care staff has access to the treatment information relevant to their roles, "Safe Plans" can be implemented for each offender living in these specialized homes. Developmentally disabled clients are typically taught to tell their staff when they are in a danger zone, and staff needs to respond to these cues by leaving the area or redirecting the client to a more appropriate focus of attention.

Families should also be alerted to the needs and issues involved in supervising the person who has a sexual behavior problem. Family support groups, parent education and Safe Plan workshops assist parents and family members in working with the person with the developmental disability while making a positive contribution to community safety efforts. Family involvement is often a positive indicator of enforcement of Safe Plans and development of support systems before discharge from the program.

SPECIALIZED STAFF TRAINING

Training of line staff in dealing with aberrant behaviors has been found to be an effective means for improving clients' behaviors (Reid, Parsons, & Green, 1989). Having well-trained staff will improve the services provided by care homes, day programs and job programs.

Behavioral strategies have been proven effective in the research. However, having such tools available are of no value if the staff does not implement the strategies (Reid et al., 1989). Staff member training affords them knowledge and skills that were previously unavailable to them. Training empowers staff members to manage significant problems specific to developmentally disabled clients for which they otherwise are unprepared.

Staff working in developmentally disabled sexual offender treatment program settings, including residential care and job programs, will need an additional focus of training beyond their training for basic residential services. Additional training topics include the following:

- Definitions and vocabulary of the Developmentally Disabled Sexual Offender Treatment Program, such as "Danger Zones," high risk factors, "Safe Plans" and interventions, line-of-sight supervision, and the concept of the zone of proximal development

- Information regarding the levels of impairment related to developmental disabilities, and those applied to the sex offender population

- Situation and behavior analysis and behavior management techniques

- Dress codes for those working with people who have sexual behavior problems

- Client needs of privacy and reasonable time alone

- Professional boundary maintenance and recognizing when a developmentally disabled client is attempting to groom staff persons or persuade them to bend the sex offender program rules or probation terms

- Issues related to the legal status of persons with developmental disabilities, i.e. self-conserved, conserved, probation requirements, etc.

- Policies related to the developmentally disabled clients' sexual expression, including prohibition of sexual or other dual relationships between staff and clients

- Observation skills and what to watch for when supervising developmentally disabled sex offender clients

- Learning styles and schemata of the developmentally disabled clients and how to meet the clients at their learning level

- The treatment team roles and communication protocols

- How to develop a sense of personalized care for the developmentally disabled clients, providing respect and dignity while holding them accountable and responsible for change

- Issues of privacy, confidentiality, and privileged information

- Issues of the developmentally disabled client's rights, civil rights, and the extent of self-determination based on the client's current legal situation and sexual proclivities

- Self-care strategies for those working with this challenging population

The Ethics of Touch: Establishing and Maintaining Appropriate Boundaries in Service to People with Developmental Disabilities is a notable, commercially available resource for staff training. It is a video and book training set available from Diverse City Press at www.diversecitypress.com.

Residential and day programs need to delineate their policies regarding touching among developmentally disabled sexual offender clients. Some agencies prohibit all touching while others allow side-hugs, hand shaking, or a hand on the shoulder. Some agencies prohibit sex between clients. Most agencies prohibit sexual activity between clients and staff.

At times, agency policies about touching and sexual behaviors may conflict with the desires of a conservator of a person with developmental disabilities. It is recommended that discussions be held with conservators at the time of placement to ascertain their input on this issue. Whether a conserved person can hug, kiss, or have sex without the consent of their conservator, and what the liabilities are for those who allow such conduct without gaining consent are frequent questions. In some cases, the non-conserved person with developmental disabilities is chargeable with a sexual crime if consent was not appropriately obtained. Line staff needs to be sensitive to these issues.

Investment in staff training allows the performance level of the culture to rise. Improving staff understanding and skills will create a higher functioning environment, which in turn would raise the standard for the social learning modeling that takes place on a daily basis. We should not expect clients and residents to rise above the level of functioning of the staff members or family members who provide much of their education through modeling appropriate behavior.

By working together, collaborative efforts offer benefits for the person with developmental disabilities as well as for community safety. Having communication systems in place, identifying roles and responsibilities of the agencies involved, having policies and protocols for risk management in the community, and specialized training empowers a more effective intervention for those with sexual behavior problems.

CHAPTER EIGHT ═══

MEASURING FAILURE & SUCCESS

WHEN discussing recidivism, the definition of what constitutes a re-offense is often raised. In a pure sense, re-offense occurs when a new sexual crime is committed. However, reporting and detecting new sex crimes are infrequent events. If rearrest for a sexual crime is the yardstick for measuring recidivism, most new crimes will be undetected. Other methods of measuring treatment efficiency need to be developed. To date, studies of treatment efficacy among mainstream offenders have not yielded consistent results (Hanson, 1997b).

Measuring within-treatment changes of dynamic risk factors has been recommended (Hanson, 1997b). Static factors cannot be changed such as an arrest record, date of birth, etc. Dynamic factors include those that are changeable. Dynamic factors include one's marital status, age, sexual preferences, effectiveness of anger management skills, use of alcohol or other drugs, and types of cognitions and/or fantasies. Testing pretreatment and posttreatment are expensive propositions that are rarely undertaken in community-based programs. Community-based programs have not been funded to be research sites, making collection of such data problematic. Ethical standards prohibit subjecting persons with developmental disabilities to experimental procedures.

Lund (1992) articulated a schema for measuring treatment outcomes for persons who have been institutionalized. Lund used the following categories of treatment outcome.

- Move to a less restrictive intervention
- Move to a less restrictive living situation
- Discharge to the community from the institution
- Reduction in maladaptive sexual behavior in the institution
- Increased grounds privileges
- Increased community or home visitation access

Lund's (1990) schema is an example of measuring intermediate factors rather than formal recidivism. The assumption is that progress in these types of domains will reduce the risk of sexual re-offense(s).

One of the problems with in-treatment measurement of progress for persons with developmental disabilities is that during treatment, they receive significant support and supervision from a number of service providers. External management and supervision may be a necessary part of the clients' lives for a significant length of time, due to their inability to function independently. Sudden removal of such intensive supports would likely undermine the emotional, behavioral and social progress the clients have made. It is difficult to measure the degree to which a particular client is "getting it" unless the full battery of assessment procedures is completed posttreatment. For those in supervised care, in vivo rehearsals observed by staff persons or clinicians may have to suffice for baseline measurement and monitoring of progress.

The DD-SORT program has formally been in independent operation for three years, although the model was partially implemented by another provider before the DD-SORT program became a separate program. The average duration of treatment in the program to date has been approximately two years, with a range of six months to three years. A small number of program graduates were from other regions, and, upon graduation, returned to their home counties. In the region that the DD-SORT program operates, limited resources for follow-up or aftercare outside the program are available. Follow-up data for program completers indicates that, to date, none have been rearrested for sexually oriented crimes. However, the number of graduates who have left residential care completely is very small, offering insignificant numbers for analysis. Unfortunately, limited data makes it difficult to generalize across settings or create subclassifications for whom certain types of services may be most appropriate.

More favorable is that the original baseline behaviors, as measured by the number of incident reports regarding problem behaviors, have reduced significantly. This would imply that the overall collaborative treatment and management strategy is helping clients to improve their functioning while in placement. Re-offense while in treatment has rarely occurred, in part due to the line-of-sight supervision. The offenses recorded are exhibitionistic behaviors and residents being sexually targeted by other offenders. Given that these clients are enrolled in a high level, line-of-sight supervision program, in-treatment re-offense behaviors may indicate a breakdown in staff attention and/or that the client failed to maintain self-control.

Another favorable note involves clients moving to less restrictive levels of care. Most of the clients entered the treatment program while placed in residential facilities with twenty-four hour awake-staff on a one to one ratio.

Community resources were developed to enable them to graduate to supervised/supported living in their own homes or apartments in the community. Being able to function within placements that are in the community without the need for ongoing therapy is seen as a measure of improvement, if not success.

Measuring progress and success in treating sexual behavior problems among people with developmental disabilities is a complicated task. From a scientific perspective, random assignment to treatment and control groups would be required to form empirically based outcome data. Other challenges involve definitions of the parameters for what constitutes recidivism, in-treatment progress, or other measures indicating the success of treatment. The ethical questions involved with random assignment for developmentally disabled persons makes it unlikely that such experimental designs would be possible. On the other hand, identifying intermediate interventions, goals, and impacts will help create a more sound science upon which to base therapeutic practices (Miner, 1997).

The hope is that this text will increase dialogue between service coordinators, residential service providers, psychotherapists and other treatment providers regarding treatment for persons with developmental disabilities who have sexual behavior problems. By further developing interagency communications, enhancing program designs, and increasing the level of awareness of these human sexuality issues more scientific data can be obtained.

REFERENCES

Abel, G. (1995). A method of organizing evaluation and treatment for sex offenders in prison and on parole. Atlanta, GA: Abel Screening, Inc.

Abel, G. (1999). The importance of meeting research standards: A reply to Fischer and Smith's articles on the Abel assessment for sexual interest. Atlanta, GA: Abel Screening, Inc.

Abel, G., Huffman, J., Warberg, B., & Holland, C. (1998). Visual reaction time and plethysmography as measures of sexual interest in child molesters. Sexual Abuse: A Journal of Research and Treatment. Vol. 10, no. 2.

Abel, G., Mittelman, & Becker, J. (1985). The effects of erotica on parapiliac's behavior. Unpublished manuscript, cited in Donnerstein, E., Linz, D. & Penrod, S. (1987) The question of pornography: Research findings and policy implications. New York: The Free Press.

Abrams, S. (1989). The complete polygraph handbook. Lexington, MA: Lexington Books.

Alloy, L., Jacobsen, N., & Acocella, J. (1999). Abnormal psychology: Current perspectives, eighth edition. Boston: McGraw-Hill College.

American Psychiatric Association (1994). Diagnostic and statistical manual of mental disorders, fourth edition. Washington, DC: Author.

Antonello, S. (1996). Social skills development: Practical strategies for adolescents and adults with developmental disabilities. Boston: Allyn & Bacon.

Association for the Treatment of Sexual Abusers (ATSA; 1997). The ATSA practitioners handbook. Beaverton, OR: Author.

Baladerian, N. (1990). Sexual and physical abuse of developmentally disabled people. Culver City, CA: Author.

Bays, L. & Freeman-Longo, R. (1989). Why did I do it again?: Understanding my cycle of problem behaviors. Brandon, VT: Safer Society Press.

Bays, L., Freeman-Longo, R., & Montgomery-Logan, D. (1990). How can I stop?: Breaking my deviant cycle. Brandon, VT: Safer Society Press.

Blasingame, G. (1994a). Sexual offender rehabilitative treatment (SORT) program manual. Unpublished. Redding, CA: Author.

Blasingame, G. (1994b). Relapse prevention for the intellectually impaired. Unpublished program document. Redding, CA: Author.

Blasingame, G. (1996). Identifying the sexual interests of sexual offenders: A look at the Abel assessment. California Coalition on Sexual Offending Newsletter. Issue #6: Spring.

Blasingame, G. (1996b). Family violence inventory-offender version (FVI-OV). Redding, CA: Author. Available: 1-800-678-0621.

Blasingame, G. (1997). Family violence inventory-victim version (FVI-VV). Redding, CA: Author. Available: 1-800-678-0621.

Blasingame, G. (1998). Suggested clinical uses of polygraphy in community-based sexual offender treatment programs. Sexual Abuse: A Journal of Research and Treatment, vol. 10, no. 1.

Blasingame, G. (1999a) Sexual habits, obsessions, and experiences survey (SHOES). Redding, CA: Author.

Blasingame, G. (1999b). Overcoming denial among sexual offenders using the Abel assessment for sexual interest and polygraphy. The Horizon Newsletter.

Blasingame, G. (2000a). Parental concern inventory-revised (PCI-R). Redding, CA: Author. Available: 1-800-678-0621.

Blasingame, G. (2000b). Developmentally disabled sexual offender rehabilitative treatment (DD-SORT) program manual. Redding, CA: Author. Available: 1-800-678-0621.

Blasingame, G. (2000c). Adult behavioral concerns inventory. Redding, CA: Author. Available: 1-800-678-0621.

Bradford, J. (1997). Medical interventions in sexual deviance. In Laws, R. & O'Donohue, W., eds. (1997) Sexual deviance: Theory, assessment, and treatment. New York: Guilford Press.

Brown, J. & Pond, A. (1999). "They just don't get it"-Essentials of cognitive-behavioral treatment for intellectually disabled sexual abusers. In Schwartz, B. ed. The sexual offender: Theoretical advances, treating special populations, and legal developments, vol. III. Kingston, NJ: Civic Research Institute.

Bumby, K. (1996). Assessing the cognitive distortions of child molesters and rapists: Development and validation of the MOLEST and RAPE scales. Sexual Abuse: A Journal of Research and Treatment, vol. 8, no. 1.

California Mental Health & Developmental Disabilities Center (CMHDDC) (1999a). Our core values. Author. Available at www.npi.ucla.edu/mmdd

California Mental Health & Developmental Disabilities Center (CMHDDC) (1999b). Eligibility criteria Author: available at www.npi.ucla.edu/mmdd

Cavanagh-Johnson, T. (1998). Child sexual behavior checklist-revised. Treatment exercises for abused children and children with sexual behavior problems. South Pasadena, CA: Author.

Cavanagh-Johnson, T. (1999). Understanding your child's sexual behavior: What's natural and healthy. Oakland, CA: New Harbinger Publications.

Check, J. & Malamuth, N. (1986). Pornography and sexual aggression: A social learning theory analysis. In McLaughlin, M. ed. (1986) Communication yearbook 9. Beverly Hills, CA: Sage, cited in Donnerstein, E., Linz, D. & Penrod, S. (1987) The question of pornography: Research findings and policy implications. New York: The Free Press.

Cipani, E., ed. (1989). The treatment of severe behavior disorders: Behavior analysis approaches. Washington, DC: American Association on Mental Retardation.

Clark, C. (1999). Specific intent and diminished capacity. In Hess, A., & Weiner, I., eds. (1999), The handbook of forensic psychology, second edition. New York: John Wiley & Sons.

Coston, L. & Lakey, J. (1999). Creative therapy with intellectually disabled male adolescent sex offenders. In Schwartz, B. ed. The sexual offender: Theoretical advances, treating special populations, and legal developments, vol. III. Kingston, NJ: Civic Research Institute.

Dacey, J. & Travers, J. (1996). Human development across the lifespan, third edition. Dubuque, IA: Brown & Benchmark Publishers.

Donnerstein, E., Linz, D. & Penrod, S. (1987) The question of pornography: Research findings and policy implications. New York: The Free Press.

Edmonson, B. & Wish, J. (1975). Sex knowledge and attitudes of moderately retarded males. American Journal of Mental Deficiency, vol. 80.

Edson, C. (1991). Sex offender treatment. Oregon Department of Corrections. Medford OR.

English, K., Pullen, S., & Jones, L. (1996). Managing adult sex offenders: A containment approach. American Probation and Parole Association. Lexington, KY.

English, K. (1998). The containment approach: An aggressive strategy for community management of adult sex offenders. Psychology, Public Policy, and Law (APA), vol. 4, no.1/2.

Everington, C. (1990). The competence assessment for standing trial for defendants with mental retardation (CAST-MR): A validation study. Criminal Justice and Behavior, Vol. 17, no. 2. (Available at: IDS Publishing, 614-885-2323)

Fava, M. (2000). Drug treatment of pathologic aggression. In Fishbein, D., ed. (2000). The science, treatment, and prevention of antisocial behaviors: Application to the criminal justice system. Kingston, NJ: Civic Research Press.

Fishbein, D., ed. (2000). The science, treatment, and prevention of antisocial behaviors: Application to the criminal justice system. Kingston, NJ: Civic Research Press.

Friedrich, W., Fisher, J., Broughton, D., Houston, M., & Shafran, C. (1998). Normative sexual behavior in children: A contemporary sample. Pediatrics, 101, 4.

Gardner, W., & Cole, C. (1989). Self-management approaches. In Cipani, E., ed. (1989). The treatment of severe behavior disorders: Behavior analysis approaches. Washington, DC: American Association on Mental Retardation.

Gordon, B. & Schroeder, C. (1995). Sexuality: A developmental approach to problems. New York: Plenum Press.

Graham, L., Smailes, A., & Gambrill, D. (undated). Sexual abuse prevention for young people with disabilities. British Columbia Ministry of Health and Ministry Responsible for Seniors, Child and Youth Mental Health Services, Sexual Abuse Interventions Program.

Haaven, J., Little, R., & Petre-Miller, D. (1990). Treating intellectually disabled sex offenders: A model residential program. Orwell, VT: Safer Society Press.

Haaven, J. & Coleman, E. (2000). Treatment of the developmentally disabled sex offender. In Laws, Hudson & Ward, eds., Remaking relapse prevention with sex offenders: A sourcebook. Thousand Oaks, CA: Sage Publications.

Hajcak, F. & Garwood, P. (1989). Quick-fix sex: Pseudosexuality in adolescents. Adolescence, 23 (92), 75-76, cited in Dacey & Travers (1996), Human development across the lifespan, third edition. Dubuque IA: Brown & Benchmark Publishers.

Handen, B. (1998). Mental retardation. In Mash, E., & Barkley, R. (1998). Treatment of childhood disorders, second edition. New York: Guilford Press.

Hanson, K. & Bussi'ere, M. (1996). Predictors of sexual offender recidivism: A meta-analysis. Ministry of the Solicitor General of Canada. Available: www.sgc.gc.ca.

Hanson, K. & Thornton, D. (1999). Static-99: Improving risk assesment for sex offenders. Ministry of the Solicitor General (Canada). Available: www.sgc.gc.ca.

Hanson, K. (1997). The development of a brief actuarial risk scale for sexual offense recidivism. Department of the Solicitor General of Canada. Available: www.sgc.gc.ca.

Hanson, K. (1997b). How to know what works with sexual offenders. Sexual Abuse: A Journal of Research and Treatment, 9, 2.

Haring, N. (1989). Foreword. In Cipani, E., ed. (1989), The treatment of severe behavior disorders: Behavior analysis approaches. Washington, DC: American Association on Mental Retardation.

Hess, A. & Weiner, I., eds. (1999). The handbook of forensic psychology, second edition. New York: John Wiley & Sons, Inc.

Hingsberger, D. (1995). Hand made love: videotape for teaching males with developmental disabilities about masturbation. Eastman, Quebec: Diverse City Press.

Hingsberger, D. (1996). Under cover dick: Teaching men with developmental disabilities about condom use. Eastman, Quebec: Diverse City Press.

Hingsburger, D., Griffiths, D., and Quinsey, V. (1991). Detecting counterfeit deviance: Differentiating sexual deviance from sexual inappropriateness. The Habilitative Mental Healthcare Newsletter, vol. 10, 9 (September).

Hingsberger, D. & Harber, M. (1998). The ethics of touch: Establishing and maintaining appropriate boundaries in service to people with developmental disabilities. Eastman, Quebec: Diverse City Press.

Hingsberger, D. & Haar, S. (2000). Finger tips: A guide for teaching about female masturbation through understanding and video. Eastman, Quebec: Diverse City Press.

Huber, C. & Baruth, L. (1987). Ethical, legal and professional issues in the practice of marriage and family therapy. Columbus, OH: Merrill Publishing Company.

Iacono, W. & Patrick, C. (1999). Polygraph ("lie detector") testing: The state of the art. In Hess, A. & Weiner, I. Eds. (1999). The handbook of forensic psychology, second edition. New York: John Wiley & Sons, Inc.

Johnson, S. & Listiak, A. (1999). The measurement of sexual preference-a preliminary comparison of phallometry and the Abel assessment. In B. Schwartz (ed.) The sexual offender: Theoretical advances, treating special populations, and legal developments, vol. III. Kingston, NJ: Civic Research Institute.

Kalal, D., Nezu, C., Nezu, A., & McGuffin, P. (1999). Cognitive distortions in sexual offenders with intellectual deficits. In Schwartz, B., ed. (1999) The sex offender: Theoretical advances, treating special populations, and legal developments, vol. III. Kingston, NJ: Civic Research Institute.

Land, W. (1995). Psychopharmacological options for sex offenders. In Schwartz, B. & Cellini, H., eds. (1995) The sex offender: Corrections, treatment and legal practice. Kingston, NJ: Civic Research Institute.

LaVigna, G., Willis, T. & Donnellan, A. (1989). The role of positive programming in behavioral treatment. In Cipani, E., ed. (1989), The treatment of severe behavior disorders: Behavior analysis approaches. Washington, DC: American Association on Mental Retardation.

Laws, R., ed. (1989). Relapse prevention with sexual offenders. New York: Guilford Press.

Laws, D.R, Hudson, S. & Ward, T. eds (2000). Remaking relapse prevention with sex offenders: A sourcebook. Thousand Oaks, CA: Sage Publications.

Laws, R. & O'Donohue, W., eds. (1997). Sexual deviance: Theory, assessment, and treatment. New York: Guilford Press.

Letourneau, E. (1999). A comparison of the penile plethysmograph and Abel assessment for sexual interest on incarcerated military sex offenders. Paper presented at the Association for the Treatment of Sexual Abusers international conference. October 1999. Orlando, FL.

Lund, C. (1992). Long-term treatment of sexual behavior problems in adolescent and adult developmentally disabled persons. Annals of Sex Research, vol. 5.

Maletzky, B. (1996). Editorial. Sexual Abuse: A Journal of Research and Treatment, vol. 8, no. 1.

Mander, A., Atrops, M., Barnes, A., & Munafo, R. (1996). Sex offender treatment program: Intial recidivism study. Alaska Department of Corrections & Alaska Justice Statistical Analysis Unit, Justice Center, University of Alaska, Anchorage.

Marlatt A. & Gordon, J., eds. (1985). Relapse prevention: Maintenance strategies in the treatment of addictive behaviors. New York: Guilford Press.

Marques, J. (1999). How to answer the question "does sex offender treatment work?". Journal of Interpersonal Violence, vol. 14, no. 4.

Marques, J., Nelson, C., Alarcon, J., & Day, D. (1999). Preventing relapse in sex offenders: What we learned from SOTEP's experimental treatment program. In Laws, R., Hudson, S., & Ward, T. (1999) Remaking relapse prevention with sex offenders: A sourcebook. Thousand Oaks, CA: Sage.

Marshall, W. (1999). Diagnosing and treating sexual offenders. In Hess, A. & Weiner, I., eds. (1999), The handbook of forensic psychology, second edition. New York: John Wiley & Sons, Inc.

Mash, E., & Barkley, R. (1998). Treatment of childhood disorders, second edition. New York: Guilford Press.

McMahon, P. & Puett, R. (1999). Child sexual abuse as a public health issue: Recommendations of an expert panel. Sexual Abuse: A Journal of Research and Treatment, 11, 4.

Melton, G., Petrila, J., Poythress, N., & Slobogin, C. (1997). Psychological evaluations for the courts: A handbook for mental health professionals and lawyers, second edition. New York: Guilford Press.

Michael, R., Gagnon, J., Laumann, E., & Kolata, G., (1994). Sex in America: A definitive survey. Boston: Little, Brown & Company.

Milner, J. & Dopke, C. (1997). Paraphilia not otherwise specified: Psychopathology and theory. In Laws, R. & O'Donohue, W., eds. (1997) Sexual deviance: Theory, assessment, and treatment. New York: Guilford Press.

Minor, M. (1997). How can we conduct treatment outcome research? Sexual Abuse: A Journal of Research and Treatment, 9, 2.

Monat, R. (1982). Sexuality and the mentally retarded. San Diego: College-Hill Press.

Morris, D. (1997). The human sexes. (videotape series). Bethesda, MD: Discovery Communications, Inc. Available: www.tlc.discovery.com.

Nelson, C., Miner, M., Marques, J., Russell, K., & Achterkirchen, J. (1988). Relapse prevention: A cognitive-behavioral model for treatment of the rapist and child molester. Journal of Social Work & Human Sexuality, Vol. 7, no. 2.

Paolucci, E., Genuis, M. & Violato, C. (1999). The effects of pornography on attitudes and behaviours in sexual and intimate relationships. National Foundation for Family Research and Education. Calgary, Alberta. Available: (403) 254-9861.

Prentky, R. & Edmunds, S. (1997). Assessing sexual abuse: A resource guide for practitioners. Brandon, VT: Safer Society Press.

Reid, D., Parsons, M., & Green, C. (1989). Treating aberrant behavior through effective staff management. In Cipani, E., ed. (1989), The treatment of severe behavior disorders: Behavior analysis approaches. Washington, DC: American Association on Mental Retardation.

Regional Residential Services Society and the Nova Scotia Department of Health (1998). Relationships & sexuality: A guide to policy for individuals with intellectual disabilities and their residential service providers. Dartmouth, Nova Scotia: Author.

Rind, B., Tromovitch, P., & Bauserman, R. (1998). A meta-analytic examination of assumed properties of child sexual abuse using college samples. Psychological Bulletin, vol. 124, no. 1.

Roesch, R., Zapf, P., Golding, S., & Skeem, J. (1999). Defining and assessing competency to stand trial. In Hess, A., & Weiner, I., eds. (1999), The handbook of forensic psychology, second edition. New York: John Wiley & Sons.

Rosenberg, M. (1999). Hidden dangers on the information superhighway. The Horizon Newsletter, vol. 1, no. 2. Available: www.angelfire.com/mi/collateral/index.html.

Ryan, G. (1999). Web of meaning: A developmental-contextual approach in sexual treatment. Brandon VT: Safer Society Press.

Ryan, G. & Lane, S. (1991). Juvenile sexual offending: Causes, consequences, and corrections. Lexington, MA: Lexington Books.

Salter, A. (1988). Treating child sex offenders and victims. Thousand Oaks, CA: Sage Publications.

Schlank, A. & Shaw, T. (1996). Treating sexual offenders who deny their guilt: A pilot study. Sexual Abuse: A Journal of Research and Treatment, vol. 8, no. 1.

Schultz, C. (2000). The challenges of treatment of developmentally disabled sex offenders. California Psychologist. December.

Schwartz, B., ed. (1999). Developmentally disabled offenders. The sexual offender: Theoretical advances, treating special populations, and legal developments, vol. III. Kingston, NJ: Civic Research Institute.

Seghorn, T. & Ball, C. (2000). Assessment of sexual deviance in adults with developmental disabilities. Mental Health Aspects of Developmental Disabilities. Vol. 3, no. 2.

Shapiro, D. (1999). Criminal responsibility evaluations: A manual for practice. Sarasota, FL: Professional Resource Press.

Sherak, D. (2000). Pharmacological treatment of sexually offending behavior in people with mental retardation/developmental disabilities. Mental Health Aspects of Developmental Disabilities. Vol. 3, no. 2.

Sobsey, D. (1994). Violence and abuse in the lives of people with disabilities. Baltimore: Paul Brookes.

Stacken, M. & Shevich, J. (1999). Working with the intellectually disabled/socially inadequate sex offender in a prison setting. In Schwartz, B. ed. The sexual offender: Theoretical advances, treating special populations, and legal developments, vol. III. Kingston, NJ: Civic Research Institute.

Stanfield (1992). LifeFacts: Sexuality education. Santa Barbara, CA: Author. Available: 1-800-421-6534.

Stanfield (1993). Circles intimacy & relationships [videotape series]. Santa Barbara, CA: Author. Available: 1-800-421-6534.

Schwartz, B., ed. (1999). The sex offender: Theoretical advances, treating special populations, and legal developments, vol. III. Kingston, NJ: Civic Research Institute.

Tough, S. & Hingsberger, D. (1999). Counseling sex offenders with developmental disabilities who deny. Mental Health Aspects of Developmental Disabilities, vol. 2, no. 3.

Vygotsky, L. (1978). Mind in society: The development of higher psychological processes. Edited by Cole, M., John-Steiner, V., Scribner, S., & Souberman, E. Cambridge, MA: Harvard University Press.

Ward, K., Trigler, J., & Pfeiffer, K. (2001). Community services, issues, and service gaps for individuals with developmental disabilities who exhibit inappropriate sexual behaviors. Mental Retardation, vol. 39, no. 1.

Williams, B., Williams, R., & McLaughlin, T. (1989). The use of token economies with individuals who have developmental disabilities. In Cipani, E., ed. (1989), The treatment of severe behavior disorders: Behavior analysis approaches. Washington, DC: American Association on Mental Retardation.

Yochelson, S. & Samenow, S. (1977). The criminal personality, volumes one & two. New York: Aronson.